ETHICS IN THE PUBLIC SERVICE

The Moral Mind at Work

ETHICS IN THE PUBLIC SERVICE

The Moral Mind at Work

Charles Garofalo
Dean Geuras

GEORGETOWN UNIVERSITY PRESS/WASHINGTON, D.C.

Georgetown University Press, Washington, D.C. 20007
©1999 by Georgetown University Press. All rights reserved.
Printed in Canada
10 9 8 7 6 5 4 3 2 1 1999

Library of Congress Cataloging-in-Publication Data

Garafalo, Charles.
    Ethics in the public service : the moral mind at work / Charles
Garafalo, Dean Geuras.
        p. cm. — (Text and teaching)
    ISBN 0-87840-736-7 (cloth). — ISBN 0-87840-737-5 (paper)
    1. Civil service ethics. 2. Public administration—Moral and
ethical aspects. I. Geuras, Dean. II. Title. III. Series.
JF1525.E8G37 1999
172'.2—dc21   99-18209
                                                              CIP

CONTENTS

INTRODUCTION

This book is for practitioners and scholars who wonder about public administration's moral center of gravity and their own identity as moral agents in the process of governance. It is for those who resist reducing the ethical to the legal and their own responsibility to the technical. It is for those who refuse to allow organizational realities to shrink their souls and demean their spirits. And, it is for those who wish to maintain their integrity and seek the public interest in the complex world of power, agendas, budgets, and pressures to get the job done.

This book is about foundations and about ethical, professional, and political judgments made on the basis of those foundations. It offers neither a blueprint nor a script, nor what is fashionable but, rather, a unified approach to reasoned, reasonable, and justifiable moral positions. It proposes an objective, integrated, and flexible ethics accessible to virtually everyone, and it presumes a willingness—even an eagerness—to try some new perspectives on old problems. Our purpose is not to provide a formula to resolve ethical dilemmas but to provide administrators a different understanding of those dilemmas that, in turn, can serve as the basis for more effective resolutions. The book's title, *Ethics in the Public Service: The Moral Mind at Work*, signifies our central goal: to introduce a new and integrated ethical perspective into public administration theory and practice.

Our work in administrative ethics has provided many rewarding contacts and conversations with colleagues, regardless of theoretical differences. Indeed, some of our richest exchanges have been with those colleagues with whom we most sharply disagree. Nevertheless, our work in administrative ethics also has revealed a major gap in the literature, namely, the absence of an explicit and fundamental ethical basis for administrative thought and action. Despite the growing volume of work in the field, its ethical assumptions and aspirations lack a firm foundation. Administrators who consult the administrative ethics literature are unable to find systematic theory and practical ethical bases for their decisions and actions. The literature, although valuable in many respects, tends to be incomplete, inconsistent and, occasionally, incoherent. Thus, this book's title symbolizes our vision of the ethical practitioner whose activities are animated by an integrated understanding of thought and action.

When we began this interdisciplinary study, we were concerned that public administration scholars appeared to apply philosophical theories without sufficient appreciation of their depth and complexity. As a result, in our view, philosophical theories tended to be accepted uncritically and were favored either for their congruence with already-held beliefs or for their apparent popularity. In either case, we saw a need to integrate philosophy more fully into public administration theory and practice.

Our first inclination was to introduce a Kantian foundation into public administration ethics because we considered Kant's value to have been overlooked—he was perceived as either obscure at best or authoritarian at worst. Gradually, however, we began to recognize connections between Kant and other ethical positions such as teleology, virtue theory, and intuitionism. We, therefore, expanded our project to include them as well as Kant. The major benefit of this expansion was our realization that these theories were not as distinctly different from each other as they are commonly supposed, and it was this realization that led us to attempt to comprehend them all as an integrated and practical whole.

Five chapters and an epilogue follow this introduction. The first chapter surveys public administration theory's chief concerns, including theory building, Minnowbrook I and Minnowbrook II perspectives, and the general reluctance of public administration scholars to provide an explicit normative theory. We conclude that scholarly culpability for this timidity extends also to philosophers who seem to be more engaged in disputing minutiae than in developing comprehensive theoretical perspectives.

Chapter 2 addresses what we term the normative paradox in contemporary public administration theory. We argue that the subjectivist viewpoint in public administration theory fails, since its insistence that administrative decisions be based on ethical values is vitiated by its resistance to providing an ethical basis for those values. We also offer a critique of the theoretical bases of subjectivism, including existentialism, phenomenology, critical theory, and postmodernism, and we attend to subjectivist concerns about the potential for objectivist authoritarianism. This chapter concludes that some of the differences between subjectivists and objectivists may be more apparent than real. It sets the stage for our argument that the dichotomies in public administration theory, such as politics and administration, the bureaucratic ethos and democratic ethos, and bureaucracy and democracy, can be reconciled by our integrated objective ethics.

Chapter 3 reviews four absolutist or objective ethical theories—intuitionism, teleology, deontology, and virtue theories—and it also summarizes the interpretations and applications of deontology, teleology, and character theories in the public administration literature. It concludes with key questions that are answered in chapter 4, which attempts to advance our understanding by unifying the four objective ethical theories into a comprehensive whole. This unification, in turn, provides a firm ethical foundation for administrative thought and action, which, we maintain, is lacking in the administrative ethics literature.

Chapter 5 represents an effort to apply this ethical foundation to the administrative setting. It examines agency and autonomy in public administration, offers a specific case to illustrate the applicability of the integrated ethical perspective, and proposes a reconciliation of both the bureaucratic ethos–democratic ethos dichotomy and the bureaucracy–democracy dilemma. Finally, in the epilogue, we briefly recapitulate the history of *Ethics in the Public Service,* draw a few parallels between academic and administrative activity, and conclude with implications for ethics education and training.

Readers of *Ethics in the Public Service* need no specialized philosophic background to grasp its substance and suggestions. It is equally accessible to professional newcomers, experienced practitioners, and scholars, its point of view is consistent with human nature, and its unified approach comports with our intellectual, emotional, and ethical need for integrated and justified thought and action. The only prerequisite for reading this book is a willingness to entertain some fresh perspectives on some old problems and to restore the connective tissue between our minds, hearts, and honor.

1

Ethical Theory in Public Administration

Contemporary American public administration theory seeks a theoretical foundation, much as a hermit crab seeks a shell, by borrowing it from another discipline such as philosophy, psychology, or sociology. Because of the foundation's alien origin, or because it is a good fit with already-held beliefs, the public administrator is reluctant to evaluate it critically but merely accepts it. Such a borrowing of theory is not necessarily inappropriate, and it may even seem prudent to employ the expertise of others. We have noticed, however, a disturbing result of this otherwise reasonable approach: The theory thus adopted is too often merely a shell. For example, although enthusiastically supporting theories that justify decision-making autonomy for the public administrator, public administration theorists refuse any formulation that would determine how that autonomy must be exercised. Ethical theories are welcome so long as they do not tell people what they should do.

William M. Dunn and Bahman Fozouni (1976) observed, two decades ago, this reluctance of the New Public Administration to be committed to a specific theoretical structure while denouncing positivism for the same offense:

Spokesmen for the New Public Administration, in seeking to criticize or discredit logical positivism or the scientific enterprise itself, share an antitheory bias manifested in imitative and unreflecting belief that paradigms are mutually exclusive and incommensurable. This has led to philosophically untenable positions of epistemological relativism, solipsism, and aesthetic romanticism (p. 7).

We do not agree completely with Dunn and Fozouni concerning a systematic antitheoretical bias, but their description of the state of public administration theory seems accurate. Unfortunately, they did little to solve the problem that they so clearly observed.

Minnowbrook I

The observations of Dunn and Fozouni can be supported by an examination of the results of the first Minnowbrook conference. For example, Michael Harmon (1972), a participant in the conference, rejects the old dogma that public officials are not to make evaluative judgments but offers no system to assist in making them. He begins a search for a theory that will "accommodate the motives and values of individual public administrators to theories of administrative responsibility" (p. 179). However, he does not inform the public administrator concerning what his or her motives should be, nor does he indicate which theories of administrative responsibility are correct and duly applicable. His attempts to respond to these issues rely on a commitment to a "new existentialism" that presumably removes the inability of the old existentialism to reduce ethical ambiguity (p. 181). However, he does not show how this reduction is accomplished. In a manner that exemplifies the problems noted by Dunn and Fozouni, Harmon finds a positive message in the old existentialists who would "refrain from defining [the values] of other people in any dogmatic fashion." Even in his more recent work (1995) in which he displays deep concern for the concept of moral responsibility, Harmon avoids "any attempt either to adjudicate disputes about the proper assignment of responsibility or to identify standards of proper conduct for public servants" (p. 201).

Yet, this reluctance to define values is precisely the problem that must be solved. It does little good merely to assert that values exist, are important, and must be applied, when no foundation for those values exists. Reference to existentialism, as John Paynter (1972) notes in his response to Harmon, does little to solve the problem since existentialism does not define ethics but only describes a state of moral freedom to which people are subject (p. 188).

Perhaps a clue to the reluctance of public administration theorists to commit themselves to a theoretical ethical structure lies in Harmon's use of the phrase "dogmatic fashion" (p. 181). He seems to assume—and in this he is probably representative of many contemporary thinkers—that any prescriptive moral theory is dogmatic. But a theory is dogmatic only if it lacks good reason. To assume that all prescriptive moral theory lacks good reason is to adopt the relativism mentioned by Dunn and Fozouni. However, if one adopts that relativism, there are no ethical matters to worry about.

Larry Kirkhart (1972), another participant in the Minnowbrook conference, relies on phenomenology, which has little more specificity than existentialism, in order to resolve ethical problems. After providing an admirable summary of philosophic and sociological theories used to form a basis for public administration, he indicates his preference for a consociated model (p. 162). According to that model, consensus within working groups of public administrators forms the basis for decision making. The consensus is more consistent with phenomenology than existentialism, because phenomenology emphasizes common agreement among the perceptions of individuals rather than absolute individual autonomy. But like existentialism, phenomenology can provide only a description of the process of moral deliberation rather than a formulation that indicates the conclusion that should be reached. Furthermore, Kirkhart gives no reason to accept phenomenology other than that it is contemporary and fits the consociated model that he favors.

At least one conference participant, George Frederickson (1972), commits himself to a specific value. He argues the New Public Administration is founded upon the notion of equity, which public administration exists to provide (p. 311). According to Frederickson, the pursuit of social equity should cause public administrators to be concerned less with the interests of the organization and more with its public responsibility. The New Public Administration thus threatens the more established bureaucratic structures that serve primarily themselves and, as a consequence, their more powerful clientele.

Admirable as Frederickson's aims may be, however, he has not provided a theory to support his value of equity. We may all approve of that value, but he gives us no formulation concerning how to adjudicate between that value and others—such as political stability, adherence to the public will, and rights of private property—that will inevitably conflict with equity. Frederickson is somewhat the reverse of Harmon and Kirkhart. They offer theory without value, whereas he offers value without theory. None offers commitment to a theory that justifies specific values.

The dilemma of the participants might be best exemplified in Philip Kronenberg's (1972) effort to provide an empirical theory but endow it with moral authority. That authority derives, according to Kronenberg, from the "participants in the political system" (p. 172). Yet, he is uncertain who those participants are. He is wary of a tyranny of the majority or of powerful, influential elites (p. 215). The question of what is meant by "the participants" may run deeper than Kronenberg acknowledges. Clearly, he means to identify a uniquely authoritative public, but does not explain whence their authority derives. To identify them as "the participants in the political system," he must specify their source of moral authority, but when asked, "What is the source of authority?" he replies, "The participants." The approach appears circular.

Kronenberg attempts to solve the dilemma not with a theory but with a collection of theories, a Public Administration Theoretical Inventory, which he defines as "a collection of empirical propositions . . . and some criteria of evaluation" (p. 224). But, here again, he leaves the critical questions unanswered. What counts as an appropriate criterion of evaluation? He can answer only that it must not be "majoritarian" or "elitist-oriented" but that it must have "political resonance" with the still unspecified public. He expects that the criterion will emerge from an empirical examination of the inventory, but he does not indicate how this emergence will take place or what moral authority such an emergence would possess. He seems to assume a theory of consensus that is little improvement over Kirkhart's consociated model.

Minnowbrook II

The Minnowbrook II contributions, as published in *Public Administration Review* (1989), which appear to be most relevant to our concerns, are the essays by John Burke and Kathryn Denhardt. Burke addresses the role of the responsible administrator in the reconciliation of the bureaucracy–democracy dilemma, while Denhardt proposes a political perspective on public administration ethics intended to reconcile the bureaucratic ethos and democratic ethos. Although both essays are provocative, we argue that they are limited with respect to the provision of an explicit ethical basis for administrative judgment and action. Nonetheless, we believe that each analysis is sufficiently substantive to warrant additional consideration as groundwork for our own point of view and for further development of our position.

Burke argues, in the context of moral duty versus institutional obligation, that some philosophers and public administration scholars tend "to treat the question of bureaucratic conduct largely as a matter of ethics and morality" and "to view the dilemmas confronting public officials as by and large resolvable by moral principles that are applicable regardless of the particular institutional setting" (p. 180). Despite the Kantianism implicit in these statements and his acknowledgment that moral duties and political and institutional obligations are mutually dependent, Burke maintains that an exclusively or even largely ethical perspective fails to provide a firm basis for understanding problems of bureaucratic conduct. He believes that many problems of bureaucratic conduct are either amoral or only tangentially ethical and that an ethical perspective is not uniform in its selection of principles to define and resolve dilemmas. More important, "[a] purely moral approach gives insufficient weight to the institutional obligations of public officials, obligations that may justifiably trump the claims of a morally inspired politics" (p. 181). Still, Burke does suggest that the questions and methods of moral philosophers are germane to reconciling the institutional and moral obligations of public administrators.

Although we will frame the issues differently, we agree with Burke that the ethical and institutional or political obligations of public administrators must be considered together. But we disagree with his depiction of some issues as either amoral or only tangentially ethical. We believe that this view perpetuates a false distinction between the moral and the technical, or the deontological and the teleological, which is familiar to students of public administration as the politics–administration dichotomy. As Robert Cleary said in his response to Burke, "I do not agree that attempts to define the responsibilities of public administrators in bridging democracy and bureaucracy must be political and institutional *rather than* moral" (p. 186). In chapter 4, we construct a unity among deontology, teleology, and character theory, which obviates the distinction drawn by Burke and other scholars, and which provides a philosophical and moral basis for the reconciliation of bureaucracy and democracy discussed by Burke as well as the bureaucratic ethos and democratic ethos discussed by Denhardt.

Denhardt notes that democratic ideals and bureaucratic ideals constitute the ethos of public administration and that "both must be accommodated in an 'ethic' of public administration" (p. 187). She argues that "the two sets of ideals are in many ways congruent," but that "they are not entirely so. Democratic ideals focus on substantive values such as individual rights, liberty, justice, and equality. Bureaucratic ideals are more instrumental, focusing on procedures and means such as efficiency, economy, standardization, hierarchical authority structures, accountability systems, impartiality, and due process" (p. 188). Denhardt also observes, however, that bureaucratic ideals are not mere instrumentalism, that in public administration "they do take on a moral character" (p. 188). Bureaucratic ideals "represent a commitment to stewardship of the public's resources through expert management to assure economy, efficiency, and effectiveness," and they "are intended to achieve a specific set of values in keeping with democratic ideals" (p. 188). Finally, in this connection, Denhardt asks why "is it not possible to subsume bureaucratic ideals under a democratic ethos?" (p. 188). She answers that "bureaucratic ideals define a good deal of the *professional* aspect of public service that distinguishes public administrators from elected and appointed officials. In other words, they offer validity and legitimacy to public administrators in a way that is separate and distinct from democratic ideals" (p. 188).

Denhardt argues, furthermore, that the public administrator "must strike an effective and justifiable balance between" bureaucratic and democratic ideals (p. 188). She notes, however, that "public administration ethics has failed to integrate effectively bureaucratic and democratic ideals" (p. 188), and in response to this failure, she offers what she calls the political perspective. This perspective associates the public administrator with the "belief system that legitimizes democratic government" (p. 189). In her view, "bureaucratic and democratic ideals should not be thought of as separate and competing perspectives but as part of one belief system that legitimates the entire political system" (p. 189). Public administrators should "have the necessary perspective to weigh all the relevant claims and to anticipate the outcomes of a particular decision" (p. 191). They must be able to exercise political judgment, which is "the living synthesis of democratic and bureaucratic ideals" (p. 191). Such judgment also "may hold the key to an ethic of public administration that makes it possible for public administrators to balance both sets of ideals in their decisions and that permits an active and ethical involvement in the political process at the same time" (p. 191). Finally, Denhardt argues that this ethic of public administration "that allows the exercise of political judgment by administrators gives legitimacy to the pursuit of democratic ideals through both political and democratic means" (p. 191).

As with Burke's essay, we find Denhardt's discussion to be a useful point of departure for the formulation of our integrated ethical position. But, like Burke, Denhardt fails to provide any explicit moral basis for the reconciliation of the dichotomy between the bureaucratic ethos and the democratic ethos. We believe that, although both essays are laudable forays into their respective topics, they do not go far enough. The underlying moral foundation for the reconciliation of bureaucracy and democracy, either on the systemic or the administrative level, remains undeveloped. We attempt to rectify this deficiency in chapter 5.

Building Public Administration Theory

Three broad themes characterize the public administration literature on knowledge acquisition: (1) subjectivism versus objectivism; (2) quantitative versus qualitative methods, particularly storytelling; and (3) the role of theory, public administration, and public administrators in society. With regard to the first theme, the standard approach among several scholars is to point out the inappropriateness or limitations of positivism for public administration research and the superiority of phenomenology, critical theory, existentialism, or postmodernism. Seldom, however, is there any mention, let alone discussion, of the moral basis of these methodologies or their associated epistemological concerns. It is as if, in their quest for alternatives to positivism and in reaction to what White and McSwain (1990) call the "technicist episteme," these scholars have uncritically adopted or borrowed philosophical perspectives, which have become their mantra, and which, apparently, in their view, require no justification or serious analysis.

We do not claim in any way that positivism should not be criticized or that phenomenology, critical theory, existentialism, or postmodernism do not merit consideration as research approaches in public administration. We merely suggest that postpositivist scholars have not delved deeply enough into their preferred alternatives and, more importantly, have not provided any ethical basis for those preferences. Positivism may, indeed, be inadequate, given its separation of fact and value, its lack of historical context, and its inattention to human purpose. Yet, simply to promote phenomenology, critical theory, existentialism, or any other approach to theory building, without specifying its ethical content, is clearly to abrogate the theorist's moral responsibility.

In his essay, "Public Administration Theory: The State of the Discipline," Robert Denhardt (1990) argues that the question of "what is acceptable, or even proper, in terms of academic research" must be addressed before we can answer the question of whether there is "any hope of developing a discipline around the concerns of those in public organizations" (p. 64). A review of the recent literature on knowledge acquisition in public administration finds a number of scholars trying to answer Denhardt's question about acceptable or proper academic research. Indeed, the literature is replete with discussions of methodology, epistemology, and the perennial theory–practice issue. What is missing, however, is conscious consideration of the underlying values or moral basis of these debates, the governing assumptions that guide the discourse and shape the outcomes. For example, in commenting on his own work in critical theory and public organizations, Denhardt contends that such an approach encompasses "self-reflection and self-critique on the part of the administrator," which "become central to organizational transformation" (p. 49). The question that Denhardt fails to address is whether organizational transformation, however defined, should be an administrative goal. It is simply assumed that organizational transformation is desirable, that critical theory will help to bring it about, and that administrators have a legitimate role in the process. Yet, without explicit and ethically grounded propositions about theory building or the theoretical enterprise as a whole, such an assumption remains unjustified and, therefore, unconvincing.

At the same time, Denhardt (1990) does suggest that public administration theorists share a moral obligation with practitioners. He argues that theorists who participate in the normative design of institutions and processes also share a responsibility for outcomes. According to Denhardt, understanding the moral implications of theory "defines the vocation and obligation of the theorist" (p. 66). We agree, but believe that the moral obligation of the theorist should be made explicit and extended to theory building and knowledge development as a whole. If public administration, including its scholarship, is, by definition, a moral activity, then theorists are obligated to clarify the ethical bases and dimensions of their theories. The methodological and epistemological debate needs to be broadened to include the implicit values and purposes in the process. Otherwise, the ethical meaning, implications, and consequences of various methodologies and epistemologies will be merely assumed and, thus, ambiguous in the acquisition, application, and assessment of knowledge and theory.

Denhardt (1990) advocates a subjectivist perspective. He borrows the definition of the subjective viewpoint from Burrell and Morgan as "focusing on and understanding of the way in which the individual creates, modifies, and interprets the world in which he or she finds himself" (pp. 52–53). Burrell and Morgan define the objective viewpoint as maintaining a belief in "universal laws which explain and govern the reality which is being observed" (p. 3). But the definitions provide a false dichotomy, which fails to consider that objective laws (e.g., moral laws) may, themselves, serve as the basis for creating, modifying, and interpreting the world. Ignoring that possibility, Denhardt immediately assumes that a focus on values is subjective. To assume so, however, is to presuppose that values have no objective basis. Under that presupposition, no normative theory can be anything but a shell, providing no explicit ethical advice.

The work of Jay White (1986) can be used to illustrate the problem. When, for example, he asserts that the interpretive model aims "to develop a more complete understanding of social relationships and to discover human possibilities" (p. 16), we are left wondering about the purpose and implications of such a goal. What may a public administrator be expected to do after attaining this more complete understanding of social relationships and human possibilities? Or is this understanding reserved for the public administration scholar whose attachment to these social relationships and human possibilities is only abstract, or indirect at best? Moreover, in reference to critical theory and, perhaps, of even greater ethical significance, White maintains that "critical research seeks to change someone's beliefs and actions in the hope of satisfying their needs and wants by bringing to awareness unconscious determinants of action or belief" (p. 16). Critique, he states, "points out inconsistencies between what is true and false, and good and bad; it compels us to act in accordance with truth and goodness" (pp. 16–17). But what is the moral basis for seeking to change someone's beliefs and actions? Where or with whom does the decision reside? On what grounds does critique compel us to act in accordance with truth and goodness?

In response to such questions, White (1992) relies heavily on scholarly consensus. He argues that consensus has generally defined truth in science through a process of practical discourse among scientists. He argues that scientific theories are not, insofar as they are theories, strictly true or false, but only more and less appropriate to the convictions of the consensus of scientists. Applying such a model to public administration, White would combine the empiricism of Kronenberg with an appeal to clear-cut authority, that is, the experts in the field.

White's analysis, however, cannot avoid the familiar problems. He does not fully explain how a model applied to scientific description of the physical world should apply to investigations of value. Even if consensus provides an appropriate manner for settling upon a scientific orthodoxy, consensus may not be appropriate for deciding normative issues. The moral dangers of mere conventionalism are self-evident. Furthermore, he overlooks an important objective aspect of scientific theory. It must be consistent with observed facts, and it must be, at least in principle, empirically testable. If the scientific model were to correlate with an approach in public administration, there would have to be established normative facts to which theory must conform and there would have to be empirical confirmation of the normative aspects of the theory. Although White is correct in pointing out that development of scientific theories is not entirely objective, he seems to suggest, wrongly, that they are almost entirely matters of subjective agreement.

Again, White, as well as other scholars writing in this vein, may be technically and even psychologically correct in their criticism of positivism and promotion of alternatives such as phenomenology and critical theory. Whether they are morally correct, however, has not been determined. Clearly, the moral basis for any research perspective requires elucidation, in order to develop a defensible framework within which research is to be designed, conducted, modified, and evaluated, and from which morally grounded theory may emerge.

The second theme—quantitative versus qualitative methods, particularly storytelling—may be considered a subset of the first. Once again, the central issue concerns the means of acquiring knowledge, but here phenomenology is applied more directly in the form of stories told by public administrators. Ralph Hummel (1990, 1991) is a leading proponent of this point of view, although others, including Jay White (1992), are active supporters as well. Although Hummel's arguments and examples relating to validity criteria, objectivity, and the managerial versus scientific worlds are generally persuasive, the moral dimension of knowledge acquisition is omitted or assumed. White, on the other hand, does intimate moral purpose in storytelling as knowledge development when he claims that, in this context, stories help to make sense of things, provide alternatives to the status quo, and inspire understanding and meaning. "Through storytelling," White says, "interpretation and critique enable social change" (p. 172). Again, however, there is no discussion of the reasons for the encouragement of social change, its scope and purpose, its methods, or its possible or preferred consequences.

The third theme related to knowledge acquisition—the role of theory, public administration, and public administrators in society—can be explored through the work of Curtis Ventriss (1987), Jay White (1992), and Richard Box (1995). Each raises a number of important issues, which are fraught with moral implications, but none fully explores or develops them. In his discussion of managerialism, for example, Ventriss suggests that public administrators must be educated in recognizing the underlying causes of social problems, as well as in the technical and professional realms. He asserts that the public is "interested in the normative issues of governmental ethics, responsibility, and accountability" (p. 30), and expresses his concern about these issues becoming "merely an afterthought in the curriculum of public administration programs" (p. 30). Furthermore, in writing of retrenchment, Ventriss indicates that it involves the question of the distribution of wealth and "how it is legitimized to the public" (p. 30). He concludes this section of his discussion by arguing that practitioners and administrative theorists have the moral obligation to speak "clearly about the meaning of social justice in an era of scarcity" (p. 31). No basis, however, is provided for this moral obligation.

In a discussion of "A Theory of Public Administration," Ventriss describes three roles for public administration in its relationship to the public. First, he suggests that public administration should become a "public social science," which critically employs several social science approaches "so that the public can better understand, debate, and discuss important policy issues" (p. 38). The goal would be to identify misinformation and distortions of data, to clarify and analyze policy choices, and to examine past policy decisions. The knowledge in which public administration as a public social science would be engaged is "knowledge that can have liberating public relevance" (p. 38).

Ventriss also argues that "public administration must begin to play a critical role in teaching citizens the principles of citizenship" (pp. 39–40). While he acknowledges the elitism and presumptuousness that might be ascribed to such a role, he observes that "public institutions already teach a kind of citizenship" (p. 40), which he claims is paternalistic and parochial. Third and last, Ventriss contends that public administration should experiment with "public learning models that can facilitate a social knowledge transfer and a disaggregate approach to public affairs" (p. 40). This involves a "client-oriented approach to policy—a perspective that acknowledges the unique needs of different publics and the necessity of defining those needs in the policy process" (p. 41). He ends with a brief discussion of ways to link citizens to the governmental process, such as a nationwide computer system, cable television, and citizen surveys. But the activist picture of the administrator as a public social scientist and teacher of citizenship lacks any moral explanation, let alone justification.

In an essay on knowledge development and public administration, White (1992) explores postpositivist modes of inquiry as well as poststructuralism and postmodernism. With respect to the role of public administration in society, he argues that the field is responsible for two main features of the modern era—the bureaucratic administrative state and reliance on technical rationality—and he asks if public administration should continue to perpetuate these features of society as the postmodern era unfolds. In this context, White asks if public administration can do anything about these challenges without being radically reconstructed. Again, however, although he cites nine implications for public administration of poststructuralism and postmodernism, the moral dimension is omitted.

In "Critical Theory and the Paradox of Discourse," Box (1995) maintains that the critical theory model seeks to minimize professional control and to maximize citizen control in the political–administrative relationship, particularly in policy making. A key component of this dynamic is the transfer of knowledge and decision-making power from politicians and administrators to citizens. Underlying the critical theory model are the goals of enlightenment and emancipation through knowledge and citizen sovereignty. Box states that "critical theory aims to create conditions in which a fully conscious public enacts change" (p. 5).

The mechanism for achieving this aim is free and open public discourse. Although Box points to established notions of citizen access to the governmental process, he provides no explicit moral basis for either critical theory or the role of the public administrator who seeks to apply it in organizational settings. In this regard, his description is akin to Ventriss's depiction of the administrator as a public social scientist and citizenship educator.

A number of public administration scholars are grappling with critical epistemological and methodological questions. Yet, despite their post-positivist and New Public Administration tendencies, their analyses fall short of addressing the fundamental moral issues underlying their methodological and epistemological concerns. Denhardt, to his credit, recognizes the moral aspects and obligations of theory and theorizing, but goes no further. In decrying positivism, he, like others, simply assumes the superior methodological and epistemological power of phenomenology and critical theory. White and Hummel, two major advocates of storytelling, also fail to examine the moral basis of their preferred alternative to positivism, and Ventriss's and Box's arguments about a theory of public administration reflect an absence of moral content as well. We must wonder, therefore, about the source or sources of this general inattention to the moral elements of theory, theory building, and knowledge acquisition.

Why is there such reluctance to provide a normative theory? There may be many reasons. First, normative values are not empirical, at least in any obvious sense. However, the absence of empirical confirmation should not bother the advocates of the New Public Administration, because they, themselves, reject the rigid empiricism of the positivists. A second possible reason is the difficulty of the subject matter. Over the centuries, no one has produced an unquestionable normative theory. But all subjects of scholarship are difficult; otherwise we would not need scholars to address them. That a subject is profound and uncertain is no reason to ignore it. There is also a third possible reason. If a correct moral theory should be found, it may be used in an overly judgmental manner. However, any moral theory must be applied humanely. As compelling as these three reasons may appear, they do not absolve theorists from the responsibility to seek an adequate normative analysis. Without one, public administration theory will remain an incomplete shell without a whole body enclosed.

The lack of such an analysis may have led to a developing withdrawal from the spirit of Minnowbrook I. Frank Marini (1994), for example, sees dangers in the allocation of too much autonomy to the public administrator.

> I fear that if we were to support some of the arguments (e.g., the Blacksburg argument) on constitutional autonomy, swing power, superior ability to represent the public and unique ability to perceive the public good, we will be very close to singing the song sheets of the likes of military potentates. . . . The notion of autonomous subservience should be subjected to some elemental criticism (p. 11).

Henry Kass (1994) sounds an equally disturbing alarm:

> Put another way, how can the public be confident in the stewardship of its employees when these employees are no longer civil servants, but public agents free to undertake and abandon their obligation based on considerations of rational self-interest or emotional attachment. It is clear that unless this issue is resolved, the feasibility and legitimacy of modern democratic governments can easily be called into question (p. 20).

The fears of Marini and Kass are legitimate, if moral autonomy is understood as independence from any objective ethics. The need for a standard to restrict administrative license is, ironically, the foundation of legitimate moral autonomy, that is, the freedom to follow a proper ethical standard rather than freedom from any ethical standard.

Yet, Marini's fear notwithstanding, the Blacksburg perspective is particularly pertinent to our final arguments concerning the dichotomous thought that has characterized the scholarship of administrative ethics as well as bureaucracy and democracy. We will maintain that, taken together, the normative goals of the Blacksburg Manifesto and what we will label our integrated objective ethics, can provide a basis for moral agency which, in turn, can contribute to the reconciliation of the bureaucracy–democracy dilemma.

The sources of the problem of morally anemic public administration theory are complex. It is tempting to blame scholars in public administration for their insufficient understanding of philosophy. If they were more philosophically grounded, they may not be as quick to accept questionable philosophic theories so uncritically. Furthermore, their understanding of the nature of philosophy may be regarded as naive. They look to contemporary philosophy to provide the latest, and therefore the most authoritative, theories, as one would look to biology to provide the latest information concerning a bacterium. Philosophy, however, is unlike the sciences. Disagreement is its essence; settled opinions are its stagnation; and in philosophy, newer is not always better.

Moreover, one might fault scholars in public administration for seeking a philosophy made to order. Supporters of the New Public Administration wished to find a theoretical justification for a system that inevitably must give public administrators moral autonomy beyond that explicitly granted in the constitutional order. At the same time, however, the scholar of public administration does not wish to recommend an ethical theory to guide the administrator; to do so would suggest imposition of the dreaded absolute. Existentialism, phenomenology, critical theory, and postmodernism fit the scholar's needs perfectly. They provide philosophic legitimacy for moral autonomy but tell us virtually nothing concerning the basis of moral judgment.

Despite such complaints, the deeper source of the problem may lie in an inability of contemporary philosophy to provide a powerful, convincing, inspiring theoretical basis for scholarly research. Through thinkers such as Plato, Aristotle, Augustine, and Aquinas, the ancient and medieval eras presented the ideal of an intelligible, orderly universe, which included values as well as facts. The prior ages of our modern era spawned humanism, rationalism, Hegelian idealism, and Marxism. The earlier years of the twentieth century were inspired by the systems of Whitehead and Dewey. Today, however, philosophy provides little inspiration or direction. Indeed, Allan Bloom (1987) questions whether contemporary philosophy stands for anything.

We do not maintain that contemporary philosophy is a wasteland. There are many brilliant philosophers, such as John Rawls, Phillipa Foot, R. M. Hare, Kurt Baier, and Bernard Williams. But they do not speak for one overpowering perspective. Consequently, no philosophical system is allowed to evolve to the level of comprehensive insight needed to inspire thinkers throughout all disciplines. Capable as they are, contemporary philosophers seem more inclined to dispute each other than to cooperate in the development of comprehensive theoretical structures.

A different approach is needed from the standpoint of both philosophy and public administration. First, the insights of philosophic perspectives should be seen in conjunction with each other rather than in internecine conflict. Second, the results of the combined insights must be demonstrated in their application to public administration practice and theory. We attempt to accomplish both of those aims in the following chapters. Our purpose is to begin a theoretical ethical dialogue within public administration theory rather than to have "the final word." A debate that roots public administration theory in philosophic soil will enrich both disciplines. In embarking on John Rohr's (1989) "high road," which bases public administration theory on moral philosophy, we invite others to join us on the journey; if they should find a better road than ours, we will gladly alter our route.

2

The Normative Paradox in Contemporary Public Administration Theory

As we noted in the previous chapter, in recent years public administration theory has been influenced, in contrasting ways, by a general rejection of logical positivism and by a general acceptance of radical subjectivism. Logical positivism, which denies the meaningfulness of all statements that are not empirically testable, is rejected because of its nullification of ethics. Meanwhile, subjectivism, which we define as the rejection of universally valid objective standards of ethics and value, is accepted. Yet, these dual influences are inconsistent with each other; subjectivism is as unable to support an objective ethics as is logical positivism.

Nevertheless, an influential group of public administration theorists supports subjectivism while rejecting the ethical void of logical positivism. These theorists, many of whom adhere to the New Public Administration as defined at Minnowbrook I, include Michael Harmon (1972), Charles Fox (1989), Robert Denhardt (1990), Jay White (1990), and Charles Fox and Hugh Miller (1995). The modern philosophical movements of existentialism, phenomenology, critical theory, and postmodernism are often cited in support of subjectivism. By no means, however, are all contemporary public administration scholars subjectivists. Michael Harmon, a defender of subjectivism, considers his position to be in the minority among public administration scholars, while remaining the prevalent view among public administration theorists. Even among them, there are numerous dissenters. George Frederickson (1972), Kathryn Denhardt (1988), Henry Kass (1994), and Frank Marini (1994), to mention a few noteworthy examples, oppose at least some of the central features of subjectivism. Still, subjectivist theories have a strong presence in contemporary public administration literature.

The purpose of this chapter is to explore the subjectivist–objectivist dimension of public administration theory, its paradoxical nature, its content, and its implications for normative thought and action. Although insisting that the public administration practitioner make decisions on the basis of ethical values, subjectivist theory provides no ethical basis for these values. As such, subjectivist ethical theory is ethical in name only. If subjectivist theory requires that ethical decisions be based on subjective grounds, it is as morally empty as logical positivism.

At the same time, however, we suspect that most theorists who espouse subjectivist theories are not so completely subjectivist as their overt beliefs suggest. We consider it more likely that the trend toward subjectivism has been motivated more by a reasonable skepticism of the more doctrinaire and authoritarian forms of ethical absolutism than by a rejection of all objective ethics and values. If their intent were to deny all normative objectivity, they would not so strongly have opposed logical positivism.

Contemporary scholars must address this paradox pertaining to the ethical content and consistency of public administration theory. Continuing to attack logical positivism is clearly of limited value. What is required, instead, is a systematic effort to clarify the subjective–objective dimension of public administration theory in order to move the dialogue forward and leave a moral legacy to our successors.

Existentialism

Existentialism, in both theistic and atheistic forms, has roots in the nineteenth century. Soren Kierkegaard (1946) is the inspiration for theistic existentialism, whose most prominent twentieth-century spokesman is Gabriel Marcel (1949), although the influence of existentialism can be seen in other theists such as Paul Tillich (1965) and Martin Buber (1956). Nietszche's (1968) atheistic philosophy is the root of recent atheistic existentialism, whose advocates include Martin Heidegger (1977), Jean-Paul Sartre (1974), and Albert Camus (1957).

Despite theological differences, modern existentialists express a common belief in radical human freedom, as expressed by Mary Warnock (1986):

> [Existentialists] aim, above all, to show people that *they are free,* to open their eyes to something that has always been true, but for which for one reason or another may not always have been recognized, namely that men are free to choose, not only what to do on a specific occasion, but what to value and how to live (pp. 1–2).

This radical freedom has both metaphysical and ethical aspects. In its metaphysical aspect, existentialism absolutely denies the determinism evident not only in earlier Calvinistic thought but also in modern behaviorism and materialism. The existentialist interprets all such deterministic theories as denials of human responsibility.

The ethical freedom of the existentialist is also absolute. The existentialist demands that each individual make his or her own ethical decisions without dependence upon moral dogmas, ethical theories, or the moral authority of other individuals. Sartre provides an example in one of his students, who had to decide whether to join a movement of anti-Nazi resistance or care for his mother, who lived alone and depended heavily upon him. Sartre (1947) could not resolve, for the student, the choice between social responsibility and individual devotion. Neither Sartre's own ethical judgments nor his vast knowledge of philosophic theory were of any avail. Ultimately, the student had to choose on the basis of his subjective feelings, which express his personal values in overt action.

For the existentialist, all ultimate values are subjective. Although individual existentialist thinkers attempt to provide a framework for decision making, they do not provide a formulation from which moral decisions can be derived logically. Christian existentialists largely agree with Kierkegaard that commitment to ultimate values requires a "leap of faith," but it is a leap precisely because it has no logical basis. Sartre argues that, in making a moral choice, one chooses for all humanity, but Sartre insists that the individual must decide what he or she considers appropriate for all of humanity. Camus, in his novel, *The Stranger*, expresses no value except assertion of one's own individually chosen values.

Response to Existentialism

Existentialism is not primarily a theory of public administration, and it is therefore dangerous to use existentialism as a basis for decisions made in public organizations. However, insofar as existentialism applies to such decisions, it provides little guidance except to assert freedom in decision making. This freedom is often cited by advocates of subjectivist theory as justification for greater autonomy for the bureaucrat, but that justification has its costs. To accept it, one must also be prepared to reject the determinism that is essential to modern behaviorism. In accepting the essence of existentialism, one must also question the notion, commonly accepted among those who look to government to solve social problems, that social conditions cause the misfortunes of individuals. Although acceptance of such existentialist beliefs may be no serious barrier, the acceptance of the radical freedom of the existentialist is perilous to the notion of public responsibility. Under the existentialist's analysis, the public official, in his or her state of ultimate freedom, may legitimately choose to reject the society, the political system, and the responsibilities of the office that he or she holds. Even an oath is not binding against this radical freedom. One could thus use political power for private values, regardless of whether they are consistent with those of the public and its charge. Those private values could range from devotion to religious ideals, chosen by a leap of faith, to ultimate egoism. Public administration theorists may be reluctant to commit themselves, either privately or publicly, to such a radical doctrine. One could imagine the reaction if public administration theorists advocated, for positions of power, individuals such as the character Merseualt from *The Stranger*.

Michael Harmon (1972) uses existentialism to support the authority of bureaucrats to make evaluative judgments but offers no system to assist in making them. Although seeking a "new existentialism" that presumably removes the ethical ambiguity (p. 181), he nevertheless praises the old existentialists who would "refrain from defining [the values] of other people in any dogmatic fashion." His existentialism affords no more ethical guidance than the discredited logical positivism.

Phenomenology

Phenomenology is another contemporary philosophic movement favored by some advocates of subjectivist theory. The roots of phenomenology extend at least to Immanuel Kant. Kant distinguished the world as it is, which he called the world of *noumena*, with the world as it appears, which he called the world of *phenomena*. The noumenal world, he insisted, could not be known. Consequently, the world of phenomena was the only knowable reality. Kant believed that all human beings perceived the phenomenal world in a similar manner, so he avoided solipsism. Nevertheless, Kant's common phenomenal world could be characterized as "intersubjective."

Phenomenology considers the phenomenal world to be the proper study of the philosopher and the scientist. Phenomenologists do not agree, however, concerning the relation between the phenomenal world and the reality beyond it. Some, like Franz Brentano (1971), distinguish the two worlds but admit that only the world of phenomena can be studied. Edmund Husserl (1964) appears uncertain concerning the relation between the two, whereas Maurice Merleau-Ponty (1973) appears to identify reality almost entirely with the phenomenal world.

Phenomenology's concern with a world that can be called "subjective" appeals to some advocates of subjectivist theory. Phenomenology is similar to existentialism in that regard, but phenomenology is not so emphatic in its assertion of freedom and individuality. While phenomenologists such as Husserl agree that each individual creates his own reality, or "lifeworld," phenomenologists leave open the possibility that groups of people may share the same intersubjective world. Even the seemingly "objective" world of science is, according to the phenomenologist, a creation out of subjective worlds. Bernard Delfgaauw (1969) provides the following analysis of Husserl's theory of science in its relation to ontology in general.

> As a method, phenomenology is a preparation for all philosophical investigation and research in the positive sciences. In examining the essence of each science, it discovers the basic structures of being of that science and thus becomes a regional ontology. The unity of these regional ontologies is given in formal ontology (p. 120).

Advocates of subjectivist theory, such as Larry Kirkhart (1972) and Jay White (1992), find this aspect of phenomenology supportive of their own theories. Kirkhart maintains that public administrators, working together, devise common group values. White favors a model according to which public administration establishes its values through a process of developing a common practical discourse among public administration scholars.

Response to Phenomenology

Like existentialism, phenomenology was not intended as a theory of public administration. Although, as a philosophic theory of ontology, phenomenology is most impressive, problems arise when it is applied in a political arena. Interpretations of phenomenology offered in support of the subjectivist theory suggest that public administrators might declare themselves a moral elite, deciding among themselves the basis of ethical political judgments without fear of contradiction on any "objective" grounds.

Reliance on phenomenology, while shifting the emphasis from individual to group decision making, does little more than existentialism in giving a basis for the decisions themselves. According to Larry Kirkhart's (1972) consociated model, consensus within working groups of public administrators forms the basis for decision making. But the model gives no information concerning how the groups can come to a correct decision. Phenomenology, the inspiration for the consociated model, is no better than existentialism at providing a basis for moral decision making. The existentialist demands that the individual make the decision, whereas the phenomenologist permits groups to make decisions, but neither the existentialist nor the phenomenologist offers a basis upon which a decision is to be made. The only difference lies in whether a decision is made by one person or by a group. The correctness of a decision, however, is not dependent on how many people make it but on the strength of the reasons behind it. The consociated model, for all its reliance on phenomenology, can describe a process but cannot provide the reasons.

Phenomenology provides a model that is not so radically individualistic as existentialism. Nevertheless, the essential problem in existentialism remains also in phenomenology: Whether individually determined or decided in groups, values are subjective. The phenomenalist's groups, like the existentialist's individuals, have no logical foundation for any moral commitment, and thus all moral commitment is ultimately arbitrary. One might even ask, "Why should I be morally committed to my group if I find its decrees morally unacceptable?"

Critical Theory

A third perspective embraced by a number of contemporary public administration scholars is critical theory. Identified with the Frankfurt

School's effort to reassess Marxist theory, critical theory, according to Joan Alway (1995), began as a theory with practical intent, which focused on the struggles of the proletariat in the capitalist production process. The role of such theory was to reflect, illuminate, and contribute to these struggles. Critical theory was seen as "interested science," as opposed to traditional theory, which according to Max Horkheimer, an early leader of the Frankfurt School, failed to recognize its own social determinants and functions. "In Horkheimer's estimation traditional theory uncritically reproduces bourgeois society" (p. 26).

Eventually, historical developments such as the defeat of working-class movements, the Stalinization of the Communist Party, and the rise of Fascism, led critical theorists to question the proletariat as the revolutionary subject. Horkheimer, in fact, in rejecting the assumption that theory originated in the struggles of the proletariat, effectively shifted theory's reference point from the interests of a specific class to the goal of social transformation. Critique was extended "beyond the bounds of political economy," liberation could no longer be regarded as only a matter of changes in production, and radical politics could no longer be conceived only in terms of class struggles (Alway, 1995, pp. 130–131).

With this more inclusive conception of radical politics, the category of potential change agents was correspondingly expanded. Now, thinkers, artists, students, and other marginalized groups became potentially important political actors. Presumably, bureaucrats could be counted among them. Political struggle was no longer seen primarily in the workplace or the ballot box. The concept of change and resistance to it grew more complex.

Herbert Marcuse's work most clearly expresses this new notion of radical politics. In Marcuse's view, oppression rather than economic exploitation provided the justification for revolutionary agency, and the development of consciousness was regarded as necessary in the process of human emancipation. Consciousness, however, was no longer associated with the proletariat, although it was still required for social transformation. "From Marx to Marcuse," Alway says, "an abiding concern is with how a 'true,' 'correct,' or 'revolutionary' consciousness is variously developed, thwarted, distorted, or realized." An underlying assumption is that there is an essential human consciousness waiting or wanting to be developed" (p. 132).

With Jurgen Habermas (1995), there is a shift from consciousness to language. The issue is no longer the development of consciousness but the development of the processes for reaching mutual understanding. For Habermas, the foundation of social analysis is the intersubjective relationship rather than the relationship between subject and object. Habermas maintains that our relationship to the world is found in linguistically mediated intersubjective relations. Furthermore, this emphasis on the intersubjective implies a different conception of action. In contrast to consciousness—in which the subject relates to the object through cognition and manipulation, resulting in an instrumental view of action—intersubjective relations are grounded in a communicative concept of action whose goal is to achieve mutual understanding of a concrete practical situation. In this connection, the meaning of emancipation changes from control over the external world to cooperation and the blending of means and ends. The ultimate goal of emancipatory politics is, according to Alway, "Unconstrained discursive will formation" (p. 135).

As a critical theorist, Habermas places heavy emphasis on reason and the three modes of reasoning that he believes are part of social discourse: instrumental reason, practical or interpretive reason, and critical reason. In Habermas's view, a theory of society must include all three and comprehend their interrelatedness. Instrumental reason, however, which is admittedly useful and which infuses modern social theory and social life, should not be considered preeminent. "To do so," he claims, "ignores or simply takes for granted the legitimacy of existing ends and means" (p. 321). Technique replaces moral purpose, bureaucracy replaces traditional, socially binding values. The result is a truncated public sphere controlled by an elite composed of business, labor, and the professions. As far as social science is concerned, it cannot be strictly neutral. Indeed, the empirical sciences serve technical interests and neglect practical and emancipatory interests. Experts and professionals are elevated, citizens and clients are subordinated, and administration replaces politics as the locus of legitimate social power and authority.

Practical or interpretive reason, according to Harmon and Mayer (1986), involves reflexivity, rules of thought and action, and choice. Although Americans tend to equate practical with technical, in Habermas's view, "practical denotes a far wider meaning that encompasses the moral choices involved in sustaining a human community" (p. 323). Habermas refers to interpretive social science as the historical–hermeneutical science, which is necessary but not sufficient for the realization of freedom. Habermas argues that interpretive reason and hermeneutical analysis do not provide a vision of the meaning of freedom or an explanation of what is required to attain it.

The third and final mode of reasoning that Habermas believes is part of social discourse is critical reason. A crucial feature of Habermas's analysis is the distinction between communicative action and discourse. The former assumes a consensus, whereas the latter questions that consensus. According to Habermas, we can determine the rationality of a consensus only with reference to the processes that created it. "The process of discourse is itself the end" (Harmon and Mayer, p. 324). Habermas's key concern, then, is discourse unfettered by asymmetries of power, an ideal speech situation that makes emancipation possible. This is the goal of critical reason.

The leading proponent of critical theory in academic public administration is Robert Denhardt. The chief themes in his work include hierarchical domination, instrumental–purposive rationality, positivism, and undistorted communication (Denhardt, 1981a; Denhardt, 1981b; Denhardt, 1984; Denhardt and Denhardt, 1979). As Harmon and Mayer have observed in reference to Denhardt: ". . . a critical approach to the theory and practice of public organizations would be concerned with exposing patterns of power and domination both within bureaucracy and in its relations with the citizens who are served by it. These patterns are mainly evident in the distortions of communication that are embedded in social institutions, such as bureaucracy, in which power asymmetries are present" (p. 327). John Forester (1983) and Richard Box (1995) would agree. Both have applied critical theory on the organizational level.

Response to Critical Theory

Much as the movement from existentialism to phenomenology signaled a shift in emphasis from individuals to groups, critical theory moves still more generally to universal consciousness reminiscent of Hegel's world spirit. However, critical theory still gives no criteria by which decisions can be made. First, decisions by individual bureaucrats cannot always wait for the world consciousness to impart its wisdom. Second, one might ask, "Is something correct simply because it is universally accepted?" Slavery was once universally accepted, but few today would approve of it. Surely, the world consciousness is more than mere public opinion; nothing that goes by the elegant description "world consciousness" could be so mundane and insipid. But what is this consciousness, how do we know it, and how do we know that it is right?

Critical theory, recognizing the fallacy of supposing that whatever is accepted ought to be accepted, proposes to reform social norms by exposing their bias. However, in proposing to better social consciousness, critical theory tacitly acknowledges that there must be something distinct from the consciousness itself to properly determine it. If some such thing exists—we may call it reason, not only because of its favorable implications but also because critical theorists themselves use it—one ought to try to discover that thing, regardless of what society thinks. Critical theory, like existentialism and phenomenology, merely describes a process but omits the essential factor that should govern the process.

Critical theory has an optimistic strain, which holds that, as time passes, society progresses toward an ideal social consciousness. This optimism, however, is a mere article of faith. The future may bring more turmoil and moral depravity than the present. (One can only shudder at the thought that the Nazis may have been more successful.) If we do not ruin ourselves, an accidental collision with a celestial body would suffice. What warrants this faith in the future?

Some critical theorists would argue that progress should not be understood so literally and temporally, but that progress is the removal of irrationalities (Marxists would say contradictions) in society. Faith in the future is, therefore, faith that society will continue to think and behave more rationally. However, such faith presupposes that reason provides the criteria for proper decision making. If so, we should look to reason itself, regardless of its claims to social acceptance and status.

Habermas, as a second-generation critical theorist, provides a bridge between Kant and critical theory. He is troubled, however, by the question that existentialism, phenomenology, and earlier critical theory fail to answer: In the context of Habermas's overall theory, that question can be stated as, "What should govern practical discourse?" If practical discourse is the ultimate appeal, nothing prevents it from being arbitrary. He attempts to give a broad response in his principle "U":

> For a norm to be valid, the consequences and side effects of its general observance for the satisfaction of each person's particular interests must be acceptable to all (p. 197).

The principle is insufficiently informative because it does not give criteria for acceptability or legitimate interest. The principle leaves open the possibility that a consensus could be reached for no better reason than reliance upon a Ouija board. Moreover, let us suppose that all members of the universe of discourse are believers in a religious caste system. Let us further assume that even members of the lowest caste agree that it is in their interest to be treated with low esteem. Should such a consensus be considered as valid as one that is more egalitarian?

Thomas McCarthy (1979) attempts to defend Habermas from the charge that his ethics of discourse permits arbitrary consensus:

> If, for example, all needs and interests are irremediably subjective, it seems that any agreement concerning them could be at best a contingent compromise among competing, ultimate irreconcilable self-interests. Habermas is naturally concerned to meet this type of objection. He argues that there are not only particular interests but common or "generalizable" interests; and it is precisely the function of practical discourse to test which are capable of being communicatively shared. . . . If the motivating force behind the agreement is a nondeceptive recognition of common needs and interests in light of an adequate knowledge of existing (and effectible) conditions, likely consequences, and so forth, what grounds could there be for denying that the agreement was rational? (pp. 314–315)

However, the problem is not one of showing why a consensus is not rational but of showing that it is rational. Since Habermas refuses to specify the ultimate, objective foundation for rational discourse, he can provide no criterion to determine what is rational and what is not. He can define rationality only by describing conditions under which it is supposed to emerge. Consequently, Habermas is forced to consider any resulting consensus to be rational by definition. He therefore begs the question.

Elsewhere, however, Habermas implies that practical discourse is subject to other, more authoritative criteria. In arguing that we should remove asymmetries of power, he presupposes, on the basis of his own ethical values, a criterion by which the quality of practical discourse should be judged. Practical discourse is, therefore, not the end in itself but must include another end, i.e., equality. We do not reject that end, but we merely point out that, since practical discourse is evaluated by it, practical discourse is subject to a higher value. Furthermore, his hope for an ideal speech situation also implies the existence of a further value. If practical discourse were the end in itself, it would be its own ideal.

Habermas's philosophical link with Kant suggests additional presupposed values. Habermas argues that, as a precondition of practical discourse, each participant in the process must accord an assumption of rationality and autonomy to each other participant. He thus appeals to a notion of logical consistency: If I am to engage in practical discourse, I must suppose that others are rational or I deny the very assumption upon which the process is based. Habermas therefore argues to a conclusion similar to Kant's categorical imperative, which accords to each person the status of an autonomous, rational end-in-itself. However, it is not clear that practical discourse requires Habermas's presupposition. Thrasymachus, in Plato's *Republic,* might argue that practical discourse reflects existing power structures and that there is no compelling reason why it should not. But even under the assumption that Habermas can logically prove that practical discourse presupposes equality, he is left with another problem. If he must justify equality by means of logic, then logic, not practical discourse, is the true final appeal. But such a justification would seem fatal to critical theory as well as to subjectivism in general. Logic can suffice as a justification only if logic is objective. Habermas is left between Scylla and Charybdis. If logic is objective, then there is an objective criterion that practical discourse must meet. If logic is not objective, then all consensus is arbitrary, and ethics is reduced to mere convention.

Postmodernism

Richard Rorty is often cited as the most prominent philosophical advocate of postmodernism. Although he appears to prefer the description "pragmatist" to "postmodernist," he defends the basic postmodernist position, and his work is often cited by postmodernists as a philosophic foundation. We begin our examination of postmodernism with an analysis of Rorty's thought, both because of his status among postmodernist scholars and because we consider him the strongest philosophical voice of the postmodernist movement. After discussing Rorty, we examine postmodernism as it is espoused by public administration scholars.

Characteristic of postmodernists, Rorty (1991) insists that there is no "skyhook" that takes us out of our subjective conditions to reveal a reality existing independently of our own minds or of other human minds (p. 13). He agrees with Hillary Putnam that there is no "God's eye standpoint" that reveals reality in itself (p. 14). Each person interprets reality in accordance with his own subjective condition. But Rorty attempts to avoid an individualistic free-for-all notion of truth. He emphasizes the social influence upon the individual and his beliefs. Truth, or what for Rorty substitutes for it, is an intersubjective agreement among the members of a community (p. 21). That intersubjective agreement permits the members of the community to speak a common language and establish a commonly accepted reality. The end of inquiry for Rorty is not the discovery or even the approximation of absolute truth but the formulation of beliefs that further the solidarity of the community or "reduce objectivity to solidarity" (p. 22). He argues that, once the notion of objective truth is abandoned, one must choose between a self-defeating relativism and ethnocentrism, neither of which can be justified in a manner that is not circular. He responds that one "should grasp the ethnocentric horn of the dilemma" and "privilege our own group" (p. 29). But it is unclear why one should grasp either horn, especially since there can be, by Rorty's own account, no rational basis for the choice.

Rorty gives few examples of how we should go about establishing this solidarity with our community, but one could imagine some. For Westerners, belief in a caste system is out of the question and belief in equality is essential. Solidarity with our society demands a breaking down of all attitudes and beliefs that lead us to treat one person as more intrinsically valuable than another. Consequently, we can at least entertain the ethical systems of Kant and Rawls, and we must support laws ensuring that no one is prevented from voting or in any other way participating as an equal in our society.

But even when we argue for such admirable values, Rorty precludes our arguing for them on the basis of their truth or objective validity, both of which he denies to be valid bases for values. Nor can we argue for them on logical grounds. To do so would be to admit objective value and truth. We must argue for them only because they increase solidarity in our community (p. 33). This means of arguing for a belief becomes especially troublesome when one considers the many different communities in one complex society such as ours. Liberals, conservatives, Christians, Jews, Muslims, capitalists, Marxists, and others live together and, on many issues, have divergent "webs of beliefs" (p. 93). How are we to converse on such issues if our aim is solidarity of each community rather than agreement based upon reasons aiming at objective truth? Does our community include all of these different beliefs or is a community defined by its beliefs?

The substitution of solidarity for truth can lead to strange results. Suppose, for example, that a patient is suffering from a potentially fatal disease that is fully curable by antibiotics. In his society, such illnesses are thought to be best treated by a witch doctor's incantations and potions. A doctor from without that society encourages him to seek conventional medical treatment, but to do so would be inconsistent with the patient's society. Would Rorty truly argue that there is no objective truth to this issue? Would he argue that we favor the conventional treatment only because we have solidarity with a different community? The issue is not which society to form solidarity with but how to prevent the reality of the patient's death.

One must wonder how public administrators would behave if they took Rorty's postmodernism seriously. Rather than basing their own moral decisions on their own reasons, public administrators would be reduced to poll watchers who followed only the wishes of the community that they consider to be their own. Rortianism would remove independent thought and replace it with "group think," with the community as the operative group.

Rorty does not claim that all communities are equal, so he might argue that the community of experts—be they physicians or public administrators—have opinions that are somehow better. But what makes one community better than another? Rorty has an answer to that question, but it does not help him in this case. For Rorty, a community is better only if it approaches his ideal more nearly. That ideal is the condition under which there is maximal voluntary agreement together with some tolerated disagreement (pp. 38–39). There is nothing in the case of the physician or the public administrator to suggest that their societies approximate that ideal. The medical community and the community of public administrators may, from time to time, be in total disagreement or be entirely intolerant of contrary opinions. Physicians and public administrators are, and should be, respected for their expertise rather than for the attitudes of the communities that they represent.

Public administrators should be warned of another possible excess that Rortian postmodernism might inspire. Rorty gives no clear definition of a community and no clear means of identifying one's own community. If public administrators consider themselves a community of their own and thus make decisions as a community, they will not only abdicate their autonomy as individuals but also risk charges of elitism. Such a remoteness from the society at large could invoke the all-too-common and familiar complaints of runaway bureacracy.

Furthermore, Rortian postmodernism is, ironically, inconsistent with the Western liberal community in which Rorty professes to belong. Let us take, for example, a very well-established practice in most Western legal systems: the protection of a jury from prejudicial influence of the society as a whole. Jurors, especially in well publicized cases, are purposely barred from communicating with their communities specifically to avoid Rortian justice. If the aim of inquiry in the legal system were solidarity with the community, jurors would be encouraged to allow the society at large to influence them. The aim of the generally accepted practice is to discover truth rather than to attain solidarity. Rorty may object that, while the application of the rules governing jury behavior may superficially conflict with community solidarity, the judicial practice of handling juries in this way has been agreed to by the community and thus expresses a solidarity in principle. However, the reason for this agreement is not to establish solidarity but to devise rules that best enable us to uncover the truth.

It may be objected that the law is a special case and should not be considered representative of truth in general. Yet, the same problem arises in broader areas as well. Consider, for example, the question often asked of public administrators, "Why do you oppose privatization?" Suppose that one answers in an honest and Rortian manner: I oppose privatization out of solidarity with the community of public administrators. That answer will and should evoke the response, "That is not a good reason but only a parochial bias." The Rortian answer would bring a negative response not only from those outside the community of public administrators but also from members of that community themselves. The person giving the answer should hardly be satisfied with it.

Rorty is left in an uncomfortable position. When one offers the best possible Rortian reasons for a belief, those reasons discredit the belief rather than support it. Knowing that such reasons would be unconvincing, the committed Rortian must give more convincing but disingenuous reasons. Thus the Rortian is reduced to a fundamental dishonesty. He can render his beliefs credible to the community only if he hides his ultimate reasons.

But if the Rortian insists that our examples are too carefully chosen and are not representative of truth or reality as they are best understood, we must ask, "Where are they understood in a Rortian, postmodernist manner?" Daily, we are concerned with matters of truth and reality. We might, for example, be concerned about the weather, likelihood of layoffs in our places of employment, or baseball scores. We may also be curious about facts that have no significant bearing on our material condition or emotional state: How old are the Rocky Mountains? How did Pluto become part of the solar system? Were there Irish monks in North America before the Vikings? Rorty's analysis applies not even remotely to any of these issues. Each is concerned with what is true and real, but none has anything to do with community solidarity. Rorty's analysis is so restricted in its application that, even if it is correct, it has no connection to truth in any ordinary sense but only in some very limited theoretical sense. This is ironic because Rorty insists that his analysis is pragmatic; it is doubly ironic when he claims to follow Wittgenstein, who warned against analyzing concepts divorced from their occurrence in ordinary language.

One might reply that our examples were ill-chosen because they do not belong in the area of beliefs that Rorty intends to be decided by community solidarity. Konstantin Kolenda attempts to support Rorty on this issue in *Rorty's Humanistic Pragmatism* (1990). He argues that the simple truths to which we refer in our examples are of a different sort from the more controversial and perhaps more general ones that Rorty declares to be functions of solidarity. These "commonsense-factual beliefs" are "unquestioned by participants in a given linguistic community" (p. 9); that is to say, they are not controversial because everyone agrees with them. But we believe that those statements are philosophically important. They invite the question, "Why does everyone agree with them?" If the answer is that they are obviously true, it suggests that there is an objective truth, and it applies to an overwhelming number of statements. If they are true only because, for some unknown reason, people decide to call them true, then they are not of a separate order at all and are subject to the same process of inquiry that Rorty applies to the more philosophically grand statements: They are, as we supposed when initially discussing them, allegedly matters expressing and promoting solidarity.

It seems that when statements are clear counterexamples to his theory that solidarity determines whatever passes for truth, Rorty or his supporters merely try to dismiss the statements as irrelevant to his main point. He places them in a different "safe" category of noncontroversial truth, drawing a clear line between the philosophical and the noncontroversial. So long as he does this, he has an escape hatch to avoid counterexamples. This also enables Rorty to evade the possibility of refutation. If an issue is controversial, its controversial nature ensures that no one possesses objective facts to decide it. Rorty can then say with confidence that it is not decided factually but by considerations of solidarity with one community or another. But if an issue is clearly decided, its noncontroversial nature makes it "nonphilosophical"; he can simply put it in the "safe" category, and the issue is thereby off-limits.

Furthermore, Rorty provides no good reason to distinguish noncontroversial from controversial statements. All statements, including these allegedly noncontroversial ones, are subject to the same arguments against objective truth as the philosophical ones. His arguments do not show that there are two kinds of truth but one. All truths for Rorty are equally lacking in objectivity.

How is Rorty led to these strange and esoteric conclusions about truth and reality? Like Habermas, Rorty relies heavily on an argument based on the pervasive influence of language:

> To say that truth is not out there is simply to say that where there are no sentences there is no truth, that sentences are elements of human languages, and that human languages are human creations.
> Truth cannot be out there—cannot exist independently of the mind—because sentences cannot so exist, or be out there (1989, p. 5).

And then, somewhat paradoxically:

> The world is out there, but descriptions of the world are not. Only descriptions of the world can be true or false. The world on its own—unaided by the describing activities of a human being—cannot (p. 5).

Rorty's argument, as so stated, is at least as old as the pre-Socratic Sophists and confuses an allegedly necessary condition with a sufficient condition. The argument may be put this way: "True" is a modifier that describes only sentences, so where there is no sentence there is no truth.

But the argument is badly flawed. Even if we grant that only sentences, linguistic enities, can be true, it does not follow that sentences or language alone are sufficient for truth. "Happy" can describe only a sentient being, but the mere existence of the sentient being does not entail that he is happy. The supposition that only sentences can be true does not remove the possibility that some other nonlinguistic condition is needed to render the sentence true.

Nor is it clear that the existence of a sentence is necessary for truth. If no language existed when dinosaurs did, we could still say that the statement "Dinosaurs exist" would have been true at the time of dinosaurs, because if a language like ours had existed, the statement, "Dinosaurs exist" would have been true. The same general argument would show that the statement would be true, in the same conditional sense, even if beings capable of language never existed. The existence of actual utterances is necessary for truth only in the technical sense in which the sound of the tree in the forest exists only when someone hears it.

There is a second discernible argument that appears, explicitly or implicitly, in several of Rorty's writings. We summarize the argument as follows:

1. All human inquiry, thought and belief occurs in language. [In Konstantin Kolenda's words, "*all* phenomena are relative to the language in which they are described." (1990, p. 9)]
2. All language is entirely culturally determined.
   Conclusion: There is no objective human inquiry, thought or belief.

Both of the premises are questionable, although the first has widespread support among Wittgensteinians and other linguistic philosophers. The second, however, upon close examination, renders the argument circular. To say that all language is entirely culturally determined is to assume that it is in no way determined by external reality. But that is precisely the issue in question.

There is no question that the concepts of truth and reality are philosphically difficult and mysterious. But so are other notions, such as matter, the Big Bang, and the line between life and death. The difficulty of a concept is not sufficient reason for supposing that it does not exist. But because of such difficulties, the Rortian postmodernist rejects the existence of truth and reality. Postmodernists are left with the problem of explaining, if there is no objective truth, why one should believe anything. Rorty's answer, community solidarity, is no solution.

Despite such deep problems in postmodernism, it appeals to some scholars in public administration. Postmodernism, according to Jay White (1992), "is the recognition that the European Enlightenment's promises of universal truth, beauty, and justice would not be realized in modern society" (p. 169). Referring to Jean-Francois Lyotard and Frederic Jameson, White discusses Lyotard's ideas of language games and their rules, which "are neither standard nor universal"; the incommensurability of language games, which "means that different types of knowledge exist"; and grand narratives that have lost their legitimacy and led to "a sense of loss and meaninglessness in the lives of the people who once believed in them."

White, then, turns to Jameson, who "argues that Westerners have lost the ability to deal with the present or the future," which he calls "pastiche," the imitation of dead styles. Jameson also alludes to schizophrenia and social fragmentation and argues that storytelling is one cure for both pastiche and schizophrenia (p. 171). Finally, White argues that postmodernism provides nine important epistemological, methdological, and ontological implications for public administration: (1) All forms of knowledge and methodologies are equal; (2) much knowledge is intended as advice, which becomes meaningful only if it is told as a story; (3) storytelling facilitates interpretation and critique which, in turn, "enable social change" (p. 172); (4) much of the knowledge in public administration is like a story; (5) "[m]ethodological principles are needed to guide narrative research in the field" (p. 173); (6) since public administration is responsible for "the bureaucratic state and the reliance on technical rationality" (p. 173), we must ask if these features of society should be perpetuated in light of postmodernism. White also claims that public administration is responsible for the fragmentation of society, and wonders whether it can do anything about it; (7) public administration's guiding narratives—the politics–administration dichotomy and the New Public Administration—must be considered in light of postmodernism; (8) Minnowbrook II demonstrated "the complex web of interconnected problems facing public administrators today" (p. 174); and (9) local problem solving in the postmodern era will proceed incrementally with problems addressed one at a time.

Charles Fox (1994) argues that the direct influence of philosophy on public administration ethics is difficult to substantiate. Moral philosophers are seldom cited in the literature, and when they are, their perspectives are not placed in any context. Moreover, Fox maintains that public administration ethics lacks the critical discourse associated with philosophical controversy. Instead, it is characterized by many atomistic views that go unchallenged and uncorrected. Anyone with a philosophical point of view must see public administration ethics as eclectic, eccentric, and undisciplined. Yet, in Fox's view, administrative ethics does have a central theme: "What unites virtually all ethical thought in public administration is the search for universal or quasi-universal *rules, standards,* or *principles* by which appropriate behavior may be deduced or judged; they are *foundational*" (p. 86). According to Fox, however, foundationalism in philosophy has increasingly been questioned by "cutting edge" philosophers.

After a brief review of teleology and deontology, Fox asserts that "[h]igher order rules are often either the actual expression, or secular equivalent of, 'because God said so' " (p. 87). This assertion is part of his broader attack on "foundational ethics," which he contends lacks credibility in the administrative setting. Earlier in his analysis, however, in regard to "the ethics of authoritative command," Fox claimed that there is a cultural lag between academic public administration and practitioners, suggesting that the orthodox paradigm has been abandoned by theorists but not by administrators. In any case, to Fox, postmodernism is a response to the "quixotic" attempt to find first principles. "Alas," he says, "push any logic to its foundation and one finds no presuppositionless presupposition; they vanish to another presupposition. We teeter on the brink of infinite regress—where the referent vanishes to reside in the purgatory of all *a priori* principles" (p. 92).

According to Fox, deontological views still can be found in public administration, namely, in the work of David Hart, Kathryn Denhardt, and John Rohr. Hart's social equity, Denhardt's universal moral order, and Rohr's regime values are cited in this connection. Fox, however, faults Denhardt because he believes that her view fails to show how it might inform the daily life of administrators. He concludes this section of his discussion by stating: "Deontological ethics . . . may be seen as shifting accountability and control from obedience to political masters to obedience to ethical principles" (p. 93).

Fox then asks where practitioners might look for guidance if foundational ethics does not ring true. We must remember, however, his earlier claim of a cultural lag between academics and practitioners, which suggested that practitioners still tend to rely on foundational ethics. That apparent inconsistency notwithstanding, Fox points to two "antifoundational" strands as possible guideposts for practitioners: the neo-Aristotelian or communitarian strand and the postmodern strand. Each, he argues, sees foundationalism as one of the more regrettable instances of modernist arrogance. Central to the critique of modernism is the arrogance of reason, which embodies Newtonian physics, the Big Clock, the language of universals or transcultural and transtemporal truths. The problem, Fox claims, is that rational arguments that aspire to universal status are based on what he calls an "Indian rope trick," by which he appears to mean that none is founded on a presuppositionless presupposition or first principle. Again, we are confronted with the prospect of infinite regress.

Fox ends his essay by stating, first, that postmodernism has yet to penetrate public administration ethics except to reinforce anti-foundationalism. The principal proponents of anti-foundationalism in public administration are Cynthia McSwain, Orion White, and Michael Harmon. Second, Fox addresses two implications from postmodernism: (1) that knowledge creation is an illegitimate exercise of power and domination; and (2) that the celebration of otherness and difference is its corrective. Postmodernists, he says, find in social realities veiled, arbitrary, and thus illegitimate exercises of power and domination. Metanarratives, as these realities are called, favor the West over the East, North over South, white over colored, male over female, developed over underdeveloped, and heterosexual over other sexual orientations. Difference and otherness are marginalized. Thus, all ethical views are totalitarian, and the remedy is to adopt an ethics of "let be." The imposition of morals is immoral, since morals are only consensual and arbitrary. Nonetheless, Fox suggests that postmodernism is also deeply contradictory, and he asks ultimately if we can let be those whose ways do not let others be. At which point, according to Fox, postmodernists will attack the law of contradiction as part of an occidental, Eurocentric, phallocentric, white power play. The coherence and significance of the postmoderist position are left unexplored.

To Fox and Hugh Miller (1995), of special significance in postmodernism is the "thinning of 'reality' or the development of *hyperreality*," which means that signs and words have become increasingly estranged from more authentic communities of discourse (p. 7). Although "[t]hicker, more robust communities of discourse do develop," they do so "only in enclaves or subcultures (a tendency referred to as *neotribalism*)" (p. 7). On the other hand, Fox and Miller (1995) describe themselves as partial postmodernists; that is, they believe that the "postmodern hypothesis" is only partially valid (p. 42). In any event, Fox and Miller provide a useful roadmap through postmodernism, including postmodernists' anti-foundationalism, their emphasis on the eclectic, the *ad hoc*, the ethically situational, and their interest in the incommensurable, the fragmentary, and the disparate. At the end of their discussion, Fox and Miller ask if postmodern conditions are insurmountable, and they conclude that as unsatisfying as hyperreality, thin national culture, and neotribalism may be, "orthodoxy and the representative democratic accountability feedback loop are more unsatisfying still . . ." (p. 69). Constitutionalism, neoinstitutionalism, and communitarianism, they maintain, would be unconvincing and misplaced "in an era hostile to canon" and in light of "citizen indifference and the questionable status of community" (p, 70).

Woller and Patterson (1997) also call for a postmodern perspective on administrative ethics in their discussion of the bureaucratic ethos and the democratic ethos, the two dominant ethical frameworks in public administration. The first is based on hierarchical control and obedience to political superiors, the second on what Woller and Patterson call "certain higher order principles embedded in the notion of democratic government" (p. 104). They argue that the reconciliation of democratic governance with bureaucratic values, which has been central to administrative theory, has tended to take one of three forms: (1) overhead democracy/authoritative command as an ideal; (2) external and internal accountability; and (3) direct links between administrators and citizens. Woller and Patterson find all three wanting because they are foundational and, therefore, recommend a postmodern or dialogic approach to administrative ethics.

Response to Postmodernism

Postmodernism may be characterized as the inevitable culmination of the trend toward subjectivism among a number of public administration scholars. Indeed, with postmodernism these scholars seem to have gone beyond subjectivism to disappointment, resignation, or, perhaps, a nihilism, in which established structures, systems, and certainties are felt as lost, meaningless, or discredited. Furthermore, postmodernist public administration scholars appear remarkably uncritical in their acceptance of the postmodernist perspective. White, for example, raises no concerns in his discussion of Lyotard and Jameson's analyses. Apparently, we are expected to agree, without question, that the grand narratives, however defined by Lyotard, have, in fact, lost their legitimacy and led to a sense of loss and meaninglessness. Or that Jameson's concept of pastiche and "Western fascination with the nostalgia film" (p. 171) is self-evident. The obvious question, in the context of Westerners' alleged inability to deal with the present or the future, is how to square that inability with America's notorious ahistorical, even anti-historical, tendency.

With reference to the first five of the nine implications for public administration, which White says flow from not only postmodernism but from postpositivism and poststructuralism as well, we can easily support storytelling as a method for developing knowledge and meaning. As to the sixth implication, however, we must demur. White asks what role public administration should play in light of the postmodern condition, particularly the problems of pastiche and schizophrenia feared by Jameson, and argues that public administration is responsible for the fragmentation of society asserted by Lyotard. Apart from the absence of any evidence to uphold these claims, we must express serious reservations about the scope of White's question. To impute societal fragmentation and, by implication, the erosion of grand narratives to public administration is drastically to redefine the role of public administration in governance, in particular, and society, in general.

With reference to the seventh, eighth, and ninth implications of postmodernism for public administration, we again note the total acceptance of so-called postmodern conditions and the putative obligation of public administration to adapt itself to those conditions. Finally, we wonder to what extent, if any, practitioners would find postmodern academic advice and storytelling applicable to their own work and organizations. Perhaps, they also would ask the postmodernist to explain why and how they should develop "ongoing local narratives about a multiplicity of local problems to avoid the meaninglessness that comes of social and psychological fragmentation" (p. 175).

Fox's (1994) comments about philosophy in public administration are both broad and questionable. The influence of analytic philosophy, in general, has waned since the Wittgensteinian fervor of the 1960s and early 1970s. Indeed, according to Allan Bloom (1987), philosophy today is so diverse that it speaks with no clear voice. With regard to "cutting edge" philosophies, we must note that philosophers are cutting many edges, and that people often consider the edge that cuts as that which cuts in a direction that they approve.

The characterization of Aristotle as anti-foundational is especially controversial. Interpretations of Aristotle are abundant and varied, ranging from Thomas Aquinas's to those of more contemporary writers. But virtually all serious interpretations recognize that Aristotle believes strongly in the intelligibility of reality. His belief in the final cause, or *telos,* of all of nature, in fact, gives all things purpose in an overall scheme. Thus, an anti-foundational interpretation of Aristotle contradicts many of his stated beliefs—more than can be included here. Suffice it to say that invoking the name of Aristotle in behalf of anti-foundationalism is like invoking the name of Karl Marx in behalf of free enterprise. But, then, Fox himself denies the law of non-contradiction, so perhaps Aristotle can be both foundationalist and anti-foundationalist simultaneously.

Fox and Miller (1995) assert that "in postmodern conditions standards are seen as arbitrary," while "modernity possessed shared standards from which truth functions could be derived" (p. 56). Postmodernism, in their view, is characterized by simulation, insincerity, and manipulation. Communication is monologic and inauthentic. Reality is virtual. Moreover, they argue that "[i]n postmodern conditions, any special pleading has equal claim to validity" (p. 60). "Orthodoxy may have needed reform, but it had legitimacy and truth value" (p. 64). "Modernity, however reified are the explanatory systems used to justify it, had more stable metanarratives, which were at least vulnerable to evidence of internal contradiction; there were truth functions available for use by opponents as well as proponents of the status quo" (p. 75). Therefore, given the express advantages of modernity, with all its flaws, we must wonder why postmodernism is more appealing, on whatever level. Indeed, we might pose the skeptic's question: If nothing is to be reified, then is postmodernism itself nothing more than a fragment of hyperreality?

Fox and Miller, finally, ask whether postmodern conditions can be surmounted. The implications of this question, in our judgment, are more than interesting. Why should postmodern conditions be surmounted? If they were surmounted, then would it mean a return to modernity? Does this question suggest that postmodernists do not quite approve of postmodern conditions and their patent dysfunctions? In the end, we maintain that the work of White and Fox and Miller reflects a critical need to revisit the issues of foundations, justifications, and, indeed, the reification of postmodernism itself. Scholars need to examine assertions such as "At an intellectual level, anything that attempts to pass itself off, in postmodern conditions, as canonical (like the founding of a constitution or some distant social contract) will be debunked, deconstructed, and dismissed" (Fox and Miller, p. 67). We should ask if the cavalier debunking, deconstructing, and dismissing of canons furthers the discourse and leads to a renewed sense of legitimacy and meaning. Lastly, we need to wonder why, even in postmodern circumstances, it is not possible, indeed even essential, to adhere to a set of fundamental moral principles that, we believe, transcend neotribalism, subcultures, and hyperreality.

The state of indeterminacy and confusion to which postmodernism leads is evident in the work of Woller and Patterson (1997). After disavowing objectivist, or "foundationalist" theories, they seek to find a solution to ethical problems in public administration on the basis of ontology. Although the subject of ontology, the study of the being or nature of things, includes such objective theorists as Plato and Aristotle, Woller and Patterson presuppose a peculiarly postmodern theory of ontology. That theory, as expressed by Derrida, provides no constant, stable, objective ontology. The best that Woller and Patterson can do with such a theory is reveal "cracks and discontinuities" in claims to objective truth, but they can provide no basis for belief or action. They are led to the point of questioning the entire concept of public administration: "The more appropriate question may be whether it is even still possible, in the light of these criticisms, to pursue public administration. Administration implies the very structure and hierarchy that our attention to ontology has called into question" (p. 113). Woller and Patterson attempt to salvage public administration by an approach that they call "hermeneutic," but they offer no recommendation concerning the content of that approach. Indeed, their conclusion is almost entirely negative. They argue that their ontology permits the discovery of "hidden assumptions behind the traditional approaches to administrative ethics." The result of this discovery, however, is not a new ethical theory but an analysis that "creates space for an understanding public administration that sees itself as a truly human activity." However, we are given no clues as to how to operate within that space or how that human activity should be conducted. Their inability to be helpful in this regard is not surprising but virtually inevitable, given postmodernist rejection of all objective truth and rationality. That rejection prevents postmodernism from either providing an ethical foundation in general or enlightening the public administrator concerned with ethical decisions.

Subjectivism and Authoritarianism

Many advocates of subjectivist theories fear authoritarianism, which they suppose to be founded upon absolutist ethics. Indeed, some objectivist theories may occasion authoritarianism, but so may subjectivist theories. Objectivism is not necessarily authoritarian and subjectivism is not necessarily anti-authoritarian. Once the false identification of objectivism with authoritarianism is removed, public administration theorists may have no need to flee to the seemingly more open-minded subjectivism.

To illustrate the broad scope of objectivist ethical theories, let us consider a variety of absolutist positions on the issue of abortion. Some absolutists may truly be authoritarian on the issue. They may maintain that abortion is always wrong, should be illegal, and should be severely penalized. Equally authoritarian would be the opposite position: that abortion is always moral and that people should be severely punished for even questioning the practice. But there are considerably less authoritarian and more common possible absolutist attitudes. The following statements express them: (1) I believe that abortion is wrong, but I do not believe that I have the moral authority to impose my position on others; (2) I am certain that abortion is wrong, but the issue is so complex that I can understand someone's disagreement with me; (3) I believe abortion is wrong but not a very serious transgression; (4) I believe that abortion is wrong, but I am not nearly so certain that it is wrong as I am that murder is wrong; (5) I believe that abortion is morally acceptable, unlike murder, which I consider morally unacceptable. In all five of the statements, an objective moral belief is expressed, though none can be considered authoritarian.

Rather than support authoritarianism, absolutism (unlike subjectivism) can provide objective grounds for anti-authoritarian beliefs. Only the absolutist can argue that moral freedom and autonomy have objective justification. For example, Kant, a most emphatic absolutist, maintains that a person can be moral only when free (1989, p. 52). Even if an objective theory would demand that a person perform a particular action, the theory may prohibit compelling the agent to perform the action. Furthermore, he describes the autonomy of the will as "The Supreme Principle of Morality" (p. 57).

History contains innumerable examples of absolutists who, on the basis of their absolute principles, defied authoritarian rule. They include Socrates, Jesus, Anne Hutchinson, Henry David Thoreau, and Mohandas Ghandi. In contrast, the subjectivist has no objective grounds to challenge authority because he has no objective grounds for any moral position. While some subjectivists may choose to defy authority, they have only personal attitudes on which to base their defiance. There is no clear difference in subjectivism between a preference for or against authoritarian rule and a preference for or against strawberry whirl ice cream. All preferences are subjective.

Indeed, for the subjectivist, a choice for authoritarianism is just as valid as a choice against it. Thrasymachus, for example, the subjectivist in Plato's *Republic,* argues that justice is merely the interest of the stronger. The earlier atomistic philosopher Democritus, also a subjectivist on moral matters, maintained that, since there is no objective standard of morality, one may as well obey the customs of his society. Again, there is no direct connection either between subjectivism and anti-authoritarianism or between absolutism and authoritarianism.

Conclusion

We believe that initiation of a serious dialogue concerning the application of ethical theory to public administration is timely. Public administration theory gains little by relying on the authority of philosophic theories that are, themselves, problematic. We have seen that existentialism, phenomenology, critical theory (even in its Habermasian form), and postmodernism are unable to establish a convincing subjectivist ethical theory. Although we applaud the efforts by public administration theorists to find alternatives to positivism, it is clear that borrowing uncritically and, indeed, superficially from philosophy is not the answer. Rather, in our view, two requirements must be met in this regard: First, we must have more realistic expectations of philosophy, especially in view of its failure to provide a powerful, convincing, and inspiring theoretical basis for contemporary scholarly research. Second, we must be willing to confront the paradoxical desire for moral autonomy and refusal to specify the source or nature of that autonomy.

It appears that reluctance to be judgmental has lapsed into a relativism in which process supersedes substance. Subjectivist theorists argue against the moral desert that is positivism, but then propose only existentialism, phenomenology, critical theory, or postmodernism, which provide no normative guidance or direction. These alternatives to positivism very nicely cater to the fear of the absolute, insofar as they provide philosophic legitimacy for moral autonomy without addressing the basis of moral judgment.

More broadly, the distinction between subjectivism and absolutism must be clearly considered. The consistent subjectivist must argue that no objective normative judgments can be made and that all allegedly moral evaluations are merely matters of personal preference and taste about which there can be objective dispute. We believe that few, if any, of those who consider themselves subjectivists would take such an ethically nihilistic stance. If they did, they would have no objection to logical positivism's reduction of ethical statements to meaninglessness. If they were to contend, as certainly they would, that slavery, racism, oppression, or authoritarianism is morally abominable, they would express an absolute judgment. To remain consistent subjectivists, they would be unable to make an objective moral distinction between Hitler and Mother Teresa.

We believe that those who appear to favor subjectivist theories actually mean to reject doctrinaire, authoritarian, uncompromising, and smugly self-assured impositions of rigid moral systems upon entire societies. We reject such impositions as well, because we find them objectively unethical. We concur with contemporary public administration theorists in their opposition to rigid and dogmatic absolutist theories, but we maintain that a rigid, dogmatic subjectivism is no better. We believe that subjectivist theorists are more enamored of the tolerant, anti-authoritarian emotive connotation of the term "subjective" than with its substance; that their aversion is more to the rigid tone of the term "absolutist" than to its essence. If we are correct, there is not so much difference as one might initially suspect between those who overtly favor subjectivism and absolutists. If so, both the alleged subjectivists and absolutists should set aside their semantic differences and proceed to develop a reasonable ethic for public administrators.

Such an ethic should interpret and apply philosophic ethics to problems that arise in public administration. Although it is impossible to provide formulaic solutions to problems such as the democratic ethos–bureacratic ethos dilemma and the problem of agency, an ethical system should at least provide general rationales that can apply to specific instances of such problems.

More is needed than mere appeal to philosophic authority. Philosophy is valuable only when it develops theories that are convincing on their own merits. Worthy philosophical ethical theories should be based upon fundamental principles that evoke virtually universal approval. Like many of the theorists discussed in this chapter, we find a good deal of value in Kant, although our interpretation of him may be different from theirs. We find Kant especially compelling because his first principle is the self-evident law of non-contradiction, to which all rational beings must adhere. We believe that, with substantial interpretation, Kant can contribute to an ethic that is at once novel and traditional. However, besides Kantianism, there are other ethical systems that can contribute to a comprehensive public administration ethic. We would do well to examine them all, including Kantianism, to determine if they can be brought to bear on public administration.

3

A Review of Absolutist Theories

In the last chapter we saw both the moral vacuity of rigid relativism and the incoherence of many theories that claim to be relativistic while making moral judgments. We are then left with the question, "If there is an absolutist basis for ethics, what is that basis and can it be justified?" It would be prudent to examine the most historically prominent attempts to answer that question. In this chapter we consider these efforts in their basic, unadorned form, and divide them into four groups: intuitionism, teleological theories, deontological theories, and character-based theories. The most highly esteemed moral philosophers in each group serve as representative examples because of the broadly recognized cogency and appeal of their arguments. We find all four groups to have serious problems but also important insights that could ultimately be combined into a comprehensive ethical system.

Intuitionism

Of the four, intuitionism is the least theoretically complex. Intuitionism is the belief that human beings possess a special faculty, or "intuition," by which they can discern the morality of an action (Blackburn, 1996, p. 198). We include, among intuitionists, those such as Francis Hutcheson and Anthony Ashley Cooper (Earl of Shaftesbury), who believe in a "moral sense" (Blackburn, 1996, p. 251). It may be argued that advocates of "situation ethics" and even some existentialists may be tacit intuitionists, although such an argument would be met with controversy. G. E. Moore (1966), the leading twentieth-century intuitionist, compared the moral sense or intuition to color perception (p. 74). He maintains that the moral quality, good, like the color yellow, is a simple property that cannot be reduced to others. One recognizes something as either yellow or non-yellow on the basis of color recognition; one does not say that something is yellow because it has a set of properties that constitute yellow, as a set of ingredients constitutes ratatouille or a set of letters constitutes the word "ratatouille." Yellow is therefore simple in the sense that is beyond analysis or more specific definition. One might argue that yellow is really a wavelength, but Moore would argue the opposite. We call light of a certain wavelength yellow because we already recognize yellow and, thereafter, find that we can associate it with a wavelength. Primitive cave dwellers could recognize the color without any understanding of wavelengths. To observe yellow requires perception rather than theory.

Likewise, for Moore, perception—or something akin to it—tells us that something is good. No complex analysis is required to recognize that Mother Teresa was morally better than Hitler; we just directly know of her vast superiority. Theorists can discuss different good aspects of Mother Teresa, but they will regard those aspects as good merely on the basis of a recognition that the property, good, belongs to those aspects. For example, we may say that her altruism was among those things that made her good, but we regard altruism as good only because we see the property, good, in altruism. But if a theory, no matter how logical, beautiful, or marvelously intricate, were to conclude that Hitler's brutality was morally better than Mother Teresa's generosity, the theory, rather than the beloved nun, would thus be impugned. Our moral intuitions provide the criteria by which we judge moral theories and are therefore the final appeal.

Despite its elegant simplicity and its appeal to the judgments of common sense, intuitionism has some serious problems. First, there is the problem of disagreement among people's moral senses. With regard to every difficult moral issue, such as abortion, capital punishment, and euthanasia, different people have entirely different intuitions. Such issues would cease to be controversial if all moral senses were in agreement. Thus, intuitionism is least helpful when a moral theory is most needed in order to adjudicate among moral claims. Secondly, even if all intuitions agreed on all issues, we could only establish the fact of human moral unanimity. That all human beings agree to something does not make it correct. If belief in slavery or racial chauvinism were ever to become universal among human beings, those practices would not thereby become morally good. Intuitionism fails to provide any good reason why the moral sense, even if it exists, should be considered reliable. Moral theory must provide a reason, rather than just a feeling or sensitivity, in support of a moral action.

Teleological Ethical Theories: Utilitarianism

Teleological ethical theories, unlike intuitionism, provide explicit reasons for moral judgments. According to a teleological ethical theory, sometimes called a "consequential ethical theory," an action is considered good or bad on account of its consequences (Blackburn, 1996, p. 77). Teleological theories designate an end or goal as the ultimate purpose of moral action. Actions that fulfill that purpose are considered good, while actions that fail to promote the goal are bad. Ethical egoism, which claims that each person should perform action to his own benefit, is a form of teleology, as is the theory that the aim of moral action is to please a deity. However, the prevalent form of teleology is utilitarianism, the belief that an action is morally good if it promotes the greatest total happiness of those whom it affects.

Jeremy Bentham (1970) and John Stuart Mill (1979) are the historically most notable utilitarians. Bentham, whose stuffed body is still on display at the University of London, where it is present for board meetings, attempted to formulate a calculus of pleasure and pain. Using the calculus, one could, at least in theory, decide among alternative courses of action: The action that provided the greatest total amount of pleasure, as best as could be calculated given the knowledge at hand, would be deemed the morally correct action. For example, let us suppose that I had one dollar to spend. If I were to use it for a cup of coffee, I would gain little pleasure; one cannot purchase very good coffee for a dollar, the pleasure would be short-lived, and the caffeine might raise my blood pressure. Perhaps more pleasure would be secured if I put the money toward the purchase of a good book. However, the dollar would constitute only a small portion of the cost of the book, and I am not sure of how much happiness the book would afford me until I read it. Perhaps a better option still might be to give the dollar to a needy person who could use it for a small amount of nourishment. Likewise, when a government has surplus funds, Bentham would apply his calculus to determine which possible allotment would maximize happiness for all.

Mill's (1979) overall views are much like Bentham's except that Mill is not so confident in the possibility of measuring happiness in quantities (p. 8). He believed that quality, which could not be measured quantitatively, was an important factor in the evaluation of happiness. Although he could offer no clear definition of quality, he would undoubtedly suppose that the sophisticated audience of the London Symphony's performance of Beethoven's Ninth Symphony would enjoy more quality of pleasure than the occupants of a mosh pit, though the latter may be enjoying a greater quantity of a lowly sort of enjoyment. The only way to decide among the qualities of pleasures, according to Mill, is to leave the choice to those who can fully appreciate both of two sources of pleasure (e.g., the earnest mosher who is also an expert on music from the classical period) (1979, p. 9).

While utilitarians differ concerning how to define or describe happiness, they agree that, whatever it is, it ought to be maximized. The traditional rules of ethics, such as "Do not murder," "Do not steal," "Do not lie," and "Do unto others as you would have them do unto you" are, for the utilitarian, good guidelines for attaining society's happiness. However, they can have exceptions in the odd cases in which the rules interfere with happiness rather than promote it. The examples in which one ought to disobey the rule against lying are familiar: Tell the guest with an ugly new dress that it looks beautiful; tell the patient in severe danger that he is looking good; keep top-secret security information hidden even at the expense of total honesty. The utilitarian, while reluctant to break moral rules in general, could consider such cases unproblematic because they would illustrate only that the rules are imperfect and limited. In those cases, violation of the rule accomplishes what adherence to the rule normally does: promote the greatest happiness.

The willingness to allow exceptions ultimately creates the challenge for the utilitarian, as well as for all teleology. Are there not some cases in which principle is more important than happiness? Let us consider, for example, the case of the Salem witches. History informs us of the results of the execution of these innocent defendants. Approximately twenty people were hanged, but, soon after, the whole ugly affair caused a reassessment of the notion of witchcraft and, as a result, the delusion was ended forever. Let us suppose that, had the witches been acquitted, Salem would have been so terrified, indignant, and vengeful that hundreds would have died in the turmoil. Would a prescient judge, knowing the relatively benign consequences of executing a few, be morally obligated to choose that option because it saves lives? For the utilitarian, even the rule "Do not execute an innocent person" can have exceptions.

Some utilitarians may protest that it would almost never be the case that, all things considered, the execution of innocents would promote the greatest happiness. One must consider the shaking of confidence in the legal system when the miscarriage of justice is discovered, the overly paternalistic tendency that would influence the judge negatively in further cases, the possibility that one of the accused might, after acquittal, prove the innocence of all to the entire populace. Yes, it is unlikely that the greatest happiness would result from such an execution. Nevertheless, it is possible, and one can easily imagine it. The utilitarian must respond to cases in which principle and utility clearly and certainly conflict and must not hide behind their improbability.

To respond to such cases, a distinction is often made between "act utilitarianism" and "rule utilitarianism" (Blackburn, 1996, pp. 335, 338). The act utilitarian maintains, as we have hitherto supposed, that happiness justifies any actions needed to produce it and that moral rules are only guidelines—albeit very reliable ones. The act utilitarian seems especially vulnerable to cases such as the witch trial. However, the rule utilitarian accords a special importance to moral rules. He argues that the rules, not actions themselves, are justified by appeal to happiness, and that, once a rule is so justified, it must be applied to all actions. For example, the rule utilitarian would argue that, if the rule "Never kill an innocent person" is universally followed, society would thereby be happier than if the rule were not in effect. Therefore, the rule utilitarian would argue that one must always follow that rule and thus acquit accused witches whom one knows to be innocent, regardless of the consequences. Thus, the rule utilitarian would appear to avoid the potential moral monstrosity that looms over act utilitarianism.

However, the avoidance of one problem leads to another. If the rule utilitarian insists that one must always follow the rule that, if universally followed, would maximize happiness, a troublesome rigidity results. It is unlikely that any such rule could exist to which one would not wish to make exceptions, especially if the exceptions maximize happiness. For example, a society that always followed the rule "Do not lie" would be happier than one that observed no such rule. Nevertheless, one would not wish to be so rigid in obedience to such a rule as to allow no exceptions. One might attempt to state the rule so as to cover such cases as politeness and national security, but no formulation could exclude all reasonable exceptions while maintaining viability. But the problem is deeper than merely a matter of formulation. If the rule utilitarian argues that the rules can be disobeyed when they clearly interfere with happiness, he would be nothing more than an act utilitarian. On the other hand if the rule utilitarian, to avoid cases such as that of the Salem witches, insists on following any rule even when it interferes with happiness, he makes obedience to rules an absolute principle that takes precedence over happiness itself. He thus is no longer a utilitarian or even a teleologist but a follower of rules, regardless of consequences. Such a position would not be teleological but, as we will see, deontological. Much of contemporary utilitarian and teleological literature is devoted to this problem, but no generally agreed-upon solution has emerged.

Deontological Ethical Theories: Kant

We are therefore naturally led to deontological theories, of which Kant's is predominant. Deontological ethical theories regard an act as morally good or bad on the basis of factors other than consequences (Frankena, 1963, p. 14). Deontological theories often cite duty to moral principles as the critical factor in rendering an act morally good. Before Kant, deontological theories were most closely associated with religious dictates such as those in the Book of Exodus. The religious deontologist would accept certain principles as sacred and thus to be followed without question. Such a religious-based deontology had two serious weaknesses. First, it appealed only to those who accepted its religious foundations. Second, it was incomplete, even from a religious standpoint. As Plato had pointed out in the dialogue *Euthyphro*, the mere fact that a deity approves moral rules does not make them necessarily valid (1910). The moral rule "Do not murder" is clearly better than "Murder as many people as possible," even if a deity prefers the latter. Presumably, the deity would choose moral laws for a good reason rather than for arbitrary or perverse reasons. But if there are good reasons to follow deontological moral rules, we human beings may be able to discover at least some of them by our own lights. Once discovered, they could stand on their own as moral rules regardless of one's religious beliefs or lack of them. Although Kant was himself a theist, his *Fundamental Principles of the Metaphysics of Morals* (1989) attempts to justify deontology on grounds independent of religious belief.

Teleologists accept moral principles as means to a higher good. Utilitarians, for example, would recognize principles such as "Do not steal," "Do not murder," and "Do unto others as you would have them do unto you" as good guides to the maximization of overall happiness. For the deontologist, however, moral rules could not be mere instruments to a higher end but must be followed for their own sake. Kant had to discover something in the nature of the rules themselves that gave them their moral authority. Ultimately, Kant discovered a rationality inherent in them such that they would appeal to all rational beings.

All rational minds reject contradictions. Try as one might, one cannot consider the statement "X is an even number," understood without ambiguity, to be both true and false simultaneously. If one were to accept contradictions, the notions of truth and falsity would lose their meaning. As Aristotle pointed out, if someone accepted contradictions, it would be of no avail to try to convince him of anything because he would have rejected one of the basic elements upon which all reasoning depends (1956, pp. 184–185).

Kant attempts to show that ill-conceived moral principles are often self-contradictory. For example, suppose one were to act according to the rule "Always lie." A lie is a false statement intended to deceive. The intent to deceive is essential to lying. Actors make innumerable false statements while performing, but they are not lies because they are intended to entertain rather than to deceive. If all people tried to lie all the time, they would be thwarted. Consider a question such as "Is the first letter of your name a vowel?" which has only two alternative answers. If the response is a falsehood, it will not deceive, because the false statement is expected. If the response is truthful, it will still not be a lie because a lie must be a false statement. The principle "Always lie" therefore cannot be followed consistently. However, the principle "Always tell the truth," although sometimes painful to follow, entails no inconsistency and is therefore logically valid.

Stealing lends itself well to Kantian analysis. Let us suppose that we consider the rule "Stealing is morally acceptable" to be a moral truth. Stealing is the voluntary appropriation of the property of another without consent. However, if stealing is morally acceptable, no moral right to property can exist. But if there is no property, there is no such thing as stealing. Thus, the principle "Stealing is morally acceptable" is inconsistent with itself and worthy of rejection. Only its negation, "Stealing is not morally acceptable," survives the test of consistency.

One of Kant's (1989) favorite examples is the deceitful promise:

> For supposing it to be a universal law that everyone when he thinks himself in a difficulty should be able to promise whatever he pleases, with the purpose of not keeping his promise, the promise itself would become impossible, as well as the end that one might have in it, since no one would consider that anything was promised to him, but would ridicule all such statements as vain pretenses (p. 40).

The deceitful promise would be absurd in two respects. First, no one aware of one's use of such a universal law would believe his or her promise. Second, a promise morally obligates someone. A putative promise that does not obligate is not really a promise.

We may apply Kant's formulation to a situation that managers often face. Consider the case of ranking a subordinate on an evaluation scale. Often, out of personal favoritism, a desire for approval, or even mere sympathy, the manager ranks subordinates higher on the scale than they deserve to be ranked. He would rank an average employee as "good," a good employee as "excellent," and an excellent employee as "superior," which is the highest rank. However, if everyone followed the universal rule "Rank each employee one level above his or her deserved rank," several problems would arise. The rule would be self-defeating. The initial purpose of the manager's inflated ranking would be unfulfilled because every candidate would enjoy the same inflated ranking. In order to maintain any advantage, the manager would be required to inflate rankings once again. But to make such practice into a universal rule would repeat the same self-defeating procedure. If the manipulation is carried to its logical conclusion, all candidates would be ranked at the highest level, and the entire system would become worthless. Thus, the rule that sought to use a system for someone's advantage would, when universalized, destroy the system and, consequently, the advantage. A Kantian would therefore conclude that, to avoid logical absurdity, one should rank employees according to their merits.

Lying, stealing, promising deceitfully, and over-evaluating employees therefore cannot be made consistent universal principles. They would contradict themselves. But one must also be consistent in the application of principles. A principle that is arbitrarily applied and ignored is no principle at all. To express this form of inconsistency, Kant gives the example of a prosperous person who acts according to a principle of egoistic self-reliance. Kant (1989) admits that, although such a principle would not necessarily contradict itself, the will that generated such a principle could find itself in a contradiction.

> For a will which resolved this would contradict itself, inasmuch as many cases might occur in which one would have need of the love and sympathy of others, and in which, by such a law of nature, sprung from his own will, he would deprive himself of all hope of the aid that he desires (p. 41).

Selfish persons would not make a universal rule to the effect that all people should behave selfishly. If they did, the selfish person who made such a rule could, and almost certainly would, find himself in the position in which he needed the altruism of others to suit his own interests. Such a rule would hinder him in his selfish pursuits. Although there may not be a strictly logical absurdity, a truly egocentric person would not will such a rule. If he is wise in his egocentricity, he would wish that others would behave altruistically while he behaved selfishly. But a rule from which he exempts himself is not a universal rule.

Public administrators are familiar with the mentality that seeks self-exemption in the many cases of the so-called NIMBY or Not In My Back Yard rule. People regard public constructions such as low-rent housing, homeless shelters, and halfway houses for recovering addicts to be worthy social projects. However, the same citizens who favor such a project often insist that it not be placed in their neighborhood. If "No project should be located in any neighborhood" were a universal rule, the same citizens would complain that the government refuses to provide needed services.

Consistency thus becomes the foundation of Kant's moral theory. To formulate the concept of consistency in common language, however, is a difficult task. Since Aristotle, philosophers have tried without complete success to formulate the notion of consistency in logic. No such formulation has proven beyond dispute. It is not surprising therefore that Kant should have difficulty in formulating the notion of consistency in application to ethics. His first formulation of what he calls the categorical imperative, or absolute command, is intended to capture that notion as it is expressed in the above examples. He states it as "Act according to a maxim that you can will to be a universal law." One cannot will a maxim to be a universal law if, like "Lie" or "Stealing is morally acceptable," the maxim is inconsistent within itself when rendered universal. In addition, one cannot will a law to be universal if one intends to make exceptions for personal advantage; by virtue of the exception, such a law would not be universal.

Kant's first formulation of the categorical imperative is reminiscent of the Golden Rule, "Do unto others as you would have them do unto you." However, while the intent of the Golden Rule may be identical to that of Kant's first formulation of his categorical imperative, the wording of it permits a corrupt interpretation. The Golden Rule appears to emphasize the interests of the agent, who wishes that others would behave toward him as he behaves toward them. If misinterpreted, the Golden Rule may be understood egocentrically.

Let us consider, for example, the case of a sadomasochist. He does unto others as he would have them do unto him. He captures unsuspecting patrons of his isolated rural gas station, forces them into a room, and assaults them with a whip. After his sadistic tendencies are satisfied and while his victims are filled with rage, he hands them the whip so that they can vent their anger and satisfy his masochistic desires. He is following the letter of the Golden Rule.

While revealing the difficulties with that common saying, the example also exposes a problem with Kant's (1989) first formulation of the categorical imperative. Although the egocentricity of that formulation is not so immediately evident, it is nevertheless present. The sadomasochist in the example could act according to the universal rule "Whip someone once a week and be whipped in return." Kant is aware of this problem and attempts to solve it in his second formulation of the categorical imperative (p. 46). But in order to understand his attempt, we should first see how one would salvage the Golden Rule from the sadomasochist example. To do so, we must recognize a distinction between means and ends in themselves.

Something is valuable only as a means if it is of value to an end or purpose other than itself. For example, a pencil has value only as a means because it is valuable only for the purpose of writing or drawing. Automobiles, at least for those of us who do not worship them, are valuable as means of comfortable and swift transportation. Money is valuable only insofar as it can purchase other things. But if all things were valuable only for the sake of other things, there would be no ultimate value, and the entire value system would collapse. One would value object A for the sake of B, which would be valuable only for the sake of C, and so on *ad infinitum*. If anything is of genuine value as a means, something must be of value in itself, regardless of its utility as a means to some other end. Kant (1989) refers to such things with such value as "ends in themselves" (p. 44).

People may differ in what they consider ends in themselves. For example, suppose that I, an artistic philistine, examine an original Rembrandt painting in the presence of an avid art-lover. I marvel at the painting because it would fit so well in any living room, and I point out that its colors would blend with any decor. When the art-lover expresses her disgust at my reduction of great art to the level of furniture decoration, I excuse my boorishness and reply that, of course, the painting is valuable because it would bring an enormous sum of money on the open market. She loses her patience and, in a scolding tone, shouts, "You have no understanding. Even if it sold for nothing, even if it adorned no one's walls, and even if, as lamentable as it would be, the entire rest of the universe were annihilated, the painting would be valuable, in and of itself, without anyone to appreciate it." For her, the painting would be an end in itself.

Few of us appreciate art so profoundly. However, we consider ourselves as having inherent value rather than merely as means. Imagine our distress if we discovered that our friends, parents, and children all valued us merely for whatever material or social benefit that we can provide them. We would be disillusioned that they did not consider us as inherently important. Unless so distraught as to reach the verge of suicide, we would, despite their callousness, continue to accord ourselves the value of an end in itself.

If we would be consistent, as Kant claims that all rational beings must be, we must accord the same value to others that we accord to ourselves. Thus, we can now state the Golden Rule's intent more appropriately. I consider myself an end in itself. Therefore, I should consider all others to be ends in themselves. The sadomasochist would not have considered his victim to be an end in himself and therefore would not have truly done unto others as he would have them do unto him.

Who are these others? Am I to consider all sentient beings ends in themselves? If so, I would have to revere roaches, rats, and rattlesnakes. Not only would I refuse to consume animals but would object to their use for medical advancement or to verify pregnancy. But Kant does not believe that I need to go that far. I can distinguish myself from them because they are not rational beings. However, if my status as a rational being accords me a special moral value, it must extend to all rational beings. Thus Kant (1989) states his second formulation of the categorical imperative as *"So act as to treat humanity, whether in thine own person or in that of any other, in every case as an end withal, and never as means only"* (p. 46.). While the first formulation more explicitly captures the concept of universality inherent in the notion of consistency, the second formulation specifies more clearly an entity that is to be valued.

Yet, one may ask whether the value placed upon rational beings may be a mere human bias. We are rational beings, so we are likely to favor ourselves and therefore choose rationality as the source of intrinsic value. But is there any good reason that rationality should be considered a basis for considering someone an end in itself?

Consideration of Kant's overall theory clarifies why one should. Only a rational being is capable of independent thought, of logical inference, and of distinguishing between the consistent and the inconsistent. Consequently, only a rational being can recognize the nature of a principle as a rule that must be universally and consistently followed. In order to be capable of moral decision and action, one must be rational. As far as we can know, lower animals are motivated entirely by drives, desires, wants, and other non-rational tendencies that Kant calls "inclinations." Not even human action is moral, according to Kant, if it is motivated by inclinations, however compatible they may be with the dictates of duty, as specified by the categorical imperative. To give money to the poor to promote one's reputation, gratify one's ego, or assuage one's conscience is ultimately self-centered and therefore, at best, morally neutral. For Kant, not even the feeling of benevolence, insofar as it is merely a feeling, counts as a moral motive. In one of Kant's most telling passages, he maintains that the best example of a truly moral act is one performed dispassionately, with not even the slightest inclination, but only out of a recognition of one's duty as a rational being (Kant, 1989, p. 16). Since only a rational being acting in a rational manner can be moral, rationality is the source of moral agency. Because rationality is such a source, it also accords a special value to those who possess it. That special value justifies consideration of rational beings as ends in themselves. According to Patrick Riley (1983), ". . . man would thus be an end in himself because he is the only being capable of conceiving and following the sole unconditional end (what ought to be) that can be known" (p. 59).

One must be careful in interpreting Kant's insistence that rational beings be considered ends in themselves rather than as means. One might mistakenly suppose that one should never employ a person to perform a service, because to do so would be to make use of the person as a means. However, Kant insists not that one never be used as a means in any respect but that one never be used solely as a means, and that his or her status as an end in itself never be compromised. One can avoid such compromise while employing people, if one adopts the correct attitude.

For example, let us consider the case of a college student who seeks employment by mowing my lawn. Suppose, first, that both of us seek to take advantage of each other. He examines my yard, decides that the job is worth twenty dollars, but supposes that because I am ignorant of the price of yard work, he can sell me his services for thirty dollars. As I see him approach my door with his lawn mower, I assume that he is desperate. I am aware that the job is worth twenty dollars, but I think that I can acquire his services for ten dollars. When we each offer our bids, they are rejected, and we engage in a bargaining process that results in an agreement that he mow my lawn for twenty dollars. While the result may be satisfactory to both of us, we each treated the other as a means rather than an end in itself.

Suppose that we had each adopted a different attitude. The student believes that he can induce me to pay thirty dollars but offers twenty because he believes it to be the fair price. He respects me as an end in itself, which is not to be used for another's unfair advantage. I believe that I can convince him to do the job for ten dollars, but, even before his offer, I resolve to give him at least twenty dollars out of respect for him as an end in itself, as he respected me. As in the previous case, the job is done for twenty dollars, but the cases are entirely different. In the first case, each of us used the other only as a means, but in the second case, each treated the other as an end in itself. Relations between employers and employees in all areas may exhibit either of the attitudes expressed in the lawn-mowing example.

This value of rational beings as ends in themselves is the foundation also of Kant's insistence on the autonomy of the human will. A person can only be autonomous, and thus the source of his or her own moral actions, if free to exercise reason. Consequently, autonomy requires freedom from control by emotions, desires, and wants. But autonomy also requires freedom from control by others. Kant's moral theory therefore requires that, if we are to treat rational beings as ends in themselves, we must leave them as free as possible to make their own moral decisions. This appeal to freedom is evident in Kant's political writings as well as in his ethical treatises.

Yet here, again, a serious problem arises for Kant. All people cannot be free in all ways at all times. Their freedoms will inevitably conflict. One person's freedom to build a home conflicts with another's freedom to live in isolation; the freedom to smoke a cigarette conflicts with the freedom of another to breathe freely; the freedom of the *laissez-faire* capitalist conflicts with the freedom of the worker to unionize or of the small business owner to maintain his means of support. Complete autonomy for all is an ideal that may well be impossible to realize.

Because of such conflict, Kant (1989) must provide yet a third formulation of his categorical imperative. A truly consistent world is one in which each person acts in accord with the "idea of the *will of every rational being as a universally legislative will*" (p. 49). He goes on to show that in such a world, the residents, who are all considered as legislators, would not allow their varied autonomous wills to contradict each other. Therefore, Kant provides a general guide to the behavior of rational beings living in societies: Act in a manner that accords with a kingdom of ends, that is, a society in which all people's ends are combined consistently (p. 51). Such a society would be one in which all people are free from material deprivation, all people are treated as equals, and all are accorded full consideration as human beings. Each resident of the kingdom behaves in a manner that takes the interests of others into full account and is obedient to their interests as well as his or her own. This ideal becomes the model upon which actions in the real world are taken. Kant's this-worldly admonition thus becomes that of acting in a manner most conducive to the ideal state.

To the public administrator, the concept of a kingdom of ends can serve as the ideal that frames the entire system of public administration. Unlike the private, profit-motivated corporation, the kingdom of ends has the public good as the ultimate aim. For Kant, that aim should be a society in which human beings function as free and equal participants in a conflict-free pursuit of their own ends. The Kantian public administrator would use such an ideal as a source of motivation and encouragement. The public organization should consider that ideal not only as a social goal toward which to advance but also as a model for its own altruistic, cooperative, rather than egoistic and conflict-ridden, structure.

It is difficult to specify the relation between Kant's ethical theory and his political theory. Some interpreters of Kant, such as Hannah Arendt (1982), maintain that he was not so interested in his political theory as in his moral theory, although her position has been strongly disputed. In some cases, his political theory, at least on its surface, appears to contradict his ethical theory. For example, he recommends obedience to the state even when it behaves in an ethically questionable manner, and he disparages revolution (Reiss, 1970, p. 30). He favors representative government over pure democracy despite the greater autonomy that the individual would seem to possess in a purely democratic state (Reiss, 1970, p. 29). Nevertheless, Kant's formulations of the categorical imperative have clear influence on his political views.

A fundamental factor in Kant's political theory is its basis in human freedom, as expressed in his second formulation of the categorical imperative. He considers government to be the creation of a tacit social contract among rational beings. Government thus acquires its legitimacy from the autonomous exercise of free agents. One of the important aims of government, according to Kant, is to create a social condition of maximal freedom for all. While laws restrict human freedom, their ultimate aim is to provide an ordered society in which freedom can be relatively and evenly distributed and promoted. His strong belief in such freedom led him to oppose inherited privileges, which restrict the freedom of those born into relative poverty at the expense of those who gained wealth and status without merit (1970, p. 152).

Even his belief in representative government finds its basis in his belief in freedom. While realizing that a representative democracy, which he prefers to call a republic, does not allow the direct participation of a pure, Athenian democracy, he fears that the latter would permit a tyranny of the majority (Reiss, 1970, p. 29). He considers representative government to be the best practical method of distributing freedom appropriately.

The third formulation of the categorical imperative, which discusses a kingdom of consistent ends, is evident in his ideal of a society of free individuals pursuing their own ends. But, although the political system can help to produce the conditions under which such an exercise of freedom can exist, morality is needed to more nearly approximate such a kingdom. The possession of freedom does not ensure that it will be used properly and that the political freedoms of individuals do not conflict. Only the respect of each individual for all others as ends in themselves can permit an ideal society. Laws and political structures can facilitate such an ideal, but it cannot be approached without the moral behavior of free citizens. Thus, Kant's moral system and his political system complement each other. Both as a society of laws and as a group of rational moral individuals, we must promote the freedom of human beings as rational agents and ends in themselves.

The ideal society, however, cannot be attained in isolation. Ultimate freedom and ultimate morality can coexist only under ideal domestic and worldwide conditions. Internally, poverty and need must be eliminated. Externally, conflicts with other societies must be removed. A world free of want thus becomes a part of a *Perpetual Peace* required for a kingdom of ends to exist (Kant, 1970, pp. 93–130).

Kant's first formulation of the categorical imperative is evident in the formulation of laws that would form the structure of a political kingdom of ends. Like the moral laws, the laws of the state must be consistent and impartial. They cannot be formulated with the intent of favoring those in power, even if the power derives from the majority. If the society is to express a consistency, it must be reflected in the laws that structure the society.

One of Kant's more specific applications of the first formulation of the categorical imperative to the rule of law is in his defense of the right to duly-earned private property. He argues that to prohibit private property is to prevent someone from putting, to his own use, something that is in itself usable. Such a prohibition would not only restrict the freedom of the individual but also entail a contradiction if rendered a universal law. Allen Rosen (1993) interprets Kant's statements on the issue in the following manner:

> . . . Kant's contention is that for practical purposes there would be a contradiction in the idea of an external object that could not be owned by someone, because such a thing would be both a usable object and an object that could not be used. But that is impossible, hence private property is necessary. (p. 20)

We thus observe the evidence of all three formulations of Kant's categorical imperative in his political theory. His second formulation, which emphasizes the moral autonomy and intrinsic value of the individual, is evident in the free creation of the social contract and the aim of the state as a provider of freedom. The third formulation, which emphasizes the concept of a kingdom of ends, expresses the ideal state. The first formulation, which emphasizes the universal consistency of law, is evident in the legal structure of the state. While Kant's political theory cannot be strictly derived from his ethical theory, and despite some possible inconsistencies between them, the ethical theory forms the general foundation for the political theory. It may be argued, further, that the most important aspect of Kant's state—its promotion of moral freedom among rational ends in themselves—is also an essential aspect of his ethical theory.

Kant's frequently alternating reference to his differing formulations of the categorical imperative, in both his ethical and political theories, may be disconcerting. When one fails or seems irrelevant, he simply supplies another on a seemingly *ad hoc* basis. Moreover, while claiming that there are three formulations, he actually gives many more; he words each a bit differently nearly every time that he cites it.

Nevertheless, Kant claims that all of his formulations of the categorical imperative are equivalent. To understand this claim of equivalence, it is important to recognize the function of a formulation of the categorical imperative: It is an attempt to specify the notion of consistency in a manner that is applicable to moral behavior. As epistemologists are aware, the concept of consistency in application to reason in general has never been formulated noncontroversially. It is not surprising that any specification of the notion of consistency with respect to ethics should be problematic. Each of Kant's formulations is admittedly limited and imperfect, but each is an attempt to say "Be consistent."

An analogy may be made with translation from one language to another. Since no two languages have vocabularies that are in one-to-one correspondence, words and phrases in one language may require translation in differing forms in another language. For example, the German word *bitte* may best be translated into English in some cases as "please" and in other cases as "excuse me." The English word *die* may best be translated into French sometimes as "mourir" and other times as "crever." Some words, such as the Greek *arete* (commonly translated as "excellence" or "virtue"), may have no precise equivalent in another language such as English. In such cases, one does the best one can with such devices as alternative translations, longer formulations, or analogous usages. The same problem often occurs when one attempts to formulate a complex idea in any language. One might understand the problem as that of translating something from a world of ideas into language, which is imperfect for the task. In trying to formulate the concept of consistency in language, Kant must make use of varied linguistic forms, but the idea that he attempts to formulate—that of consistency—remains the same. The Golden Rule was also a flawed such attempt, although Kant would say that it was more deeply flawed than any of his own.

The categorical imperative is, therefore, "Be consistent," however that admonition may be specified to capture its intent in any specific case. Yet, a problem attaches to its status as "categorical." A categorical impera- tive is an absolute command, as opposed to a hypothetical imperative, which is a conditional command (Kant, 1989, p. 33). If all of the laws of morality are absolute, they would admit of no exceptions. Kant therefore may be interpreted as suggesting that it would never be morally accept- able to lie, even to save an innocent life from a murderer, to protect national secrets, or to encourage a critically ill patient. The rigidity that teleologists tried to resist becomes the curse of the Kantian deontologist. Exception to a moral rule could be justified only on the basis of a higher consideration, but there can be no consideration higher than that of morality. If exceptions were to be allowed, the moral imperative would be treated as hypothetical—as something that can be discarded under spe- cial conditions—rather than categorical. The problem becomes more profound still when one notices the potential for conflict between rules. For examples, one might interpret informing a murderer of his potential victim's location as such a conflict. To lie would violate the rule against lying, but to tell the truth would be to become an accomplice in the breaking of the rule "Do not murder." In another case, an impoverished person might be confronted by the option of stealing or letting his family starve. While there is clearly a rule against stealing, there appears also to be a rule that a parent should do whatever is necessary to ensure the survival of his or her children; such a rule appears to be implicit in one's status as a parent. If the parent steals, he breaks one rule, but if he refrains from stealing, he breaks another. These "damned if you do and damned if you don't" situations are especially troublesome for Kant because they suggest that, despite his heavy reliance upon the notion of consistency, his entire system may contradict itself.

Despite the possible problems with Kant's theory, it has had an immeasurable influence on modern ethical thought. Marcus Singer (1961), for example, attempts to derive a rational morality from the "generalization argument," which he defines as an argument of the form: "If everyone were to do that, the consequences would be disastrous" (p. 4). The argument is supplemented by the "generalization principle," *what is right (or wrong) for one person must be right (or wrong) for any similar person in similar circumstances*" (p. 5). Singer's aim is to establish the tenability of a rational, impartial ethic based on those generalized formulations, when they are properly understood. Although they are not identical in their wording to Kant's categorical imperative, they exhibit much of its essence as expressed in its first formulation, "Always act according to a maxim that you could will to be a universal law."

The debt that John Rawls owes to Kant is also significant. Rawls (1971) argues in favor of the theory that members of a society enter into a tacit social contract under a "veil of ignorance," a condition under which "no one knows his place in society, his class position or social status, nor does anyone know his fortune in the distribution of natural assets and abilities, his strength, and the like" (p. 137). The veil also hides even one's conception of the good and special psychological propensities. As Rawls himself notes, the veil of ignorance produces the state of impartial, rational, moral autonomy that Kant intended to capture in his categorical imperative. A person operating under such a veil would treat all people affected by his or her decisions as ends in themselves, because he or she could hold the position of any one of them (p. 252). Rawls argues that those operating behind the veil of ignorance would naturally adopt two "principles of justice": (1) equality in the assignment of basic rights and duties, and (2) social and economic inequalities are just only if they result in compensating benefits for everyone, and in particular for the least advantaged members of the society (p. 14). While the second may be somewhat controversial, Rawls claims that both express Kant's categorical imperative in their implication that persons act in their nature as free and equal rational beings (p. 253).

Deontology and Teleology in Public Administration

Deontology and teleology figure prominently in both public administration ethics theory and practice. Indeed, Darrell L. Pugh (1991) argues that "the principal frameworks for approaching public management ethics: bureaucratic ethos and democratic ethos" (p. 10) are teleological and deontological, respectively. Bureaucratic ethos, according to Pugh, "employs instrumental rationality, and is predicated on the values of capitalism and a market society," while democratic ethos "is based on substantive rationality, and emanates from classical values of the state and higher law" (p. 26). The main values of bureaucratic ethos are efficiency, efficacy, expertise, loyalty, and accountability; for democratic ethos, the main values are regime values, citizenship, public interest, and social equity (Pugh, 1991).

In a similar vein, Fox (1994) argues that the classical model of public administration embodies principles of hierarchy, efficiency, and the politics–administration dichotomy. It is a utilitarian system in which bureaucrats are not to exercise independence of thought or action. It is clearly akin to Pugh's bureaucratic ethos. On the other hand, Fox considers the deontological perspective, citing Kant, and suggests that David K. Hart, Kathryn Denhardt, and John Rohr represent the deontological position in public administration—Hart with his emphasis on social equity, Denhardt with her notion of a universal moral order, and Rohr with his regime values. In the end, however, Fox finds both teleology and deontology wanting, contending that they do not ring true in contemporary or postmodern society, that one presupposition follows another, leading to infinite regress, and that they are irreconcilable.

Pugh (1991), as well as Woller and Patterson (1997), also notes the hoary debate between deontology and teleology and observes that their reconciliation is highly problematic. Woller and Patterson (1997) suggest that "attempts to reconcile the two ethoses have tended to fall into one of three approaches" (109). The first approach supports the command model of bureaucratic ethos; the second "combines the notions of external and internal ethical accountability"; and the third supports a muscular democratic ethos in which citizens and administrators are directly and intimately connected. Woller and Patterson conclude that foundationally driven efforts to reconcile deontology and teleology have failed because they have asked the wrong questions. The right questions, in their view, would be both ontological and anti-foundational. The reconciliation of the bureaucratic and democratic ethos will be considered in chapter 5.

Other public administration scholars, such as Mary Guy (1991), Carol Lewis (1991), and George Frederickson (1997), observe distinct teleological and deontological components in contemporary public administration but describe them as in a mutual compromise. Guy argues that, in the United States government, services are grounded in a utilitarian concept but guided by the deontological notions of equality, freedom, and the right to property. In her estimation, public administrators in that environment "ethically satisfice," which suggests a compromise that permits "satisfaction of ethical parameters at a minimally acceptable level" (p. 187). According to Guy (1991), "[e]thical satisficing preempts the single-minded pursuit of either deontological or utilitarian ethics by blending the promotion of both means and ends" (p. 189).

Lewis (1991) argues that ethical reasoning is grounded in common sense as well as deontology and teleology. She argues, however, that American democracy has been unable or unwilling to reconcile the deontological and teleological traditions or choose between them.

Therefore, American ideology accommodates both. The Bill of Rights represents the deontological concept of underlying rules, while American culture and politics represent teleology's utilitarian principle as expressed, for example, in the widespread use of cost–benefit analysis.

Frederickson (1997) describes the world of the public administrator as "unrelentingly teleological," a world in which the public administrator practices "bounded ethics," and yet a world of "civic virtue, honesty, procedural fairness, equity, and human dignity" (pp. 169–170). In this environment, the public administrator strives for decision-making effectiveness by trying to balance daily concern for consequences with permanent concern for principles. According to Frederickson, "[e]xplicit standards of right and wrong are a defining feature of American government" (p. 168). Despite this unrelentingly teleological world and within the limits of organizational purpose and funding, the career administrator is "almost always honest, virtuous, procedurally fair, and efficient" (p. 170).

Several other public administration scholars, such as Debra Stewart (1984) and Kathryn Denhardt (1988), recognize the distinction between teleology and deontology in theory but notice their confusion in practice. Stewart (1984), for example, suggests that two distinctively different ethical systems give rise to two ethical standards guiding action: deontological ethics, which asserts that certain features of acts render them good or bad irrespective of consequence (e.g., promise keeping and truth telling); and teleological or utilitarian ethics, which sees an act as right if it produces a greater balance of good over evil. Although she contends that deontology and teleology are different ethical systems, Stewart points out that practice does bring them together.

> Most managers are neither pure deontologists, nor pure utilitarians, but rather operate according to a kind of ethical pluralism. Guided by this synthesis of moral systems, managers typically might conclude that the moral reason for or against some action resides in its consequences, while the rationale for or against other actions stem from

their being a kind required or prohibited by duty. When acting out of ethical pluralism, managers need to develop a sensitive moral judgment, for often one must apply both sorts of moral reasoning to the same actions. It might be that the consequences of some action would be so bad that it should not be undertaken even though one has a *prime facie* obligation to do it (p. 20).

Denhardt (1988) also refers to two general approaches to understanding or thinking about the moral order: a deontological approach, which focuses on universal rules that serve as guides for moral action and provide good reasons for making a decision, and a teleological approach, which focuses on the consequences of actions as the determining factor of whether the actions are good or bad. According to Denhardt, "[t]hese two approaches to understanding the moral order are important to the study of administrative ethics because the way one thinks about the moral order determines what one considers ethical, and how one makes judgments about actions" (p. 44). She suggests that, if there are universal moral principles that administrators are to observe, then one set of implications for administrative ethics follows. "If, on the other hand, the moral order is that which can be judged only by the aggregate utilities associated with the outcomes of a decision, then the administrator needs to use a different set of skills and measures in determining what is 'right'" (p. 53). Finally, Denhardt says that, because philosophers have not agreed on how to think about morality and the good, "it is unlikely that the ambiguity associated with these two ways of thinking will be resolved in a framework for understanding administrative ethics" (p. 53).

A third group of public administration scholars, such as Ralph Chandler (1994) and Gerald Pops (1994), notice that teleology and deontology may not be so distinct as they have been commonly assumed. Chandler (1994) suggests that a discussion of deontology is impossible without also discussing "the other side of the same ethics coin" (p. 147). In his view, an issue may be unique or so profound in teleological terms that the practitioner has no choice but to review the deontological principle implicit in routine norms of conduct. Chandler maintains that the everyday world of the practitioner is built around the principles, precepts, and regulations that deontological ethics encourages and sometimes prescribes, and that psychologically most people prefer to work in deontologically unambiguous circumstances. As a practical matter, organizations must appeal to the deontological consciences of their members because they have no better way to defend the organization's reputation, implying a blending of deontology and teleology. Chandler concludes that "[d]eontological ethics will maintain the notions of right and wrong for their serviceable value, but the wise citizen will remember that universal obligation attaches not to particular judgments of conscience but to acts willing both the present and the consequential good" (p. 155).

The last public administration scholar to be considered is Pops (1994), who observes that "[a]lthough it is possible (and even logical) to think of a consequence as including the attainment of a *moral* value (such as keeping promises, being fair, or insuring broad participation), we conventionally think about the *act* of serving moral values as performing duties or observing principles, not seeking consequences. To do otherwise would virtually destroy the distinction drawn in philosophy between teleology and deontology" (p. 157). He notes that, since politics is preeminently about values, "public administration cannot be a simple matter of following deontological rules and seeking teleological efficiency" (p. 161). He suggests, therefore, that public administrators function in a highly political environment in which power, conflict, and accountability are continuing concerns. It is an environment in which ends and means intersect, a world in which even those who claim to be concerned only about doing their duty will often make decisions on the basis of consequence. According to Pops, "[r]esults matter, even to deontologists" (p. 161).

All of the theories that we have so far considered have had problems. Intuitionism gives no explicit moral rules and thus is prone to subjectivity. Teleology seems to pay insufficient respect to moral rules, while deontology appears to apply them too rigidly. There is also a fourth class of theories, character-based theories, which we will now consider.

Character-Based Theories

According to character-based theories, also known as virtue ethics theories, the morality of an action is determined by the character trait that the act exhibits. These theories take "the notion of virtue as primary, rather than a view either of the 'good', for the sake of which we act, or of duty, law or reason thought of as providing rules for action . . ." (Blackburn, 1996, p. 394). For example, a character-based theory would consider the act of wanton stealing wrong because it expresses a selfish disregard for the property and well-being of others. Similarly, the character-based theorist would approve of one's contributions of large sums of money to the poor if the act bespoke a kindly nature, as opposed to self-aggrandizement. Character-based theorists maintain that the person, rather than the action, is the object of moral evaluation.

Aristotle is the prime example of a character-based theorist. He regarded all good character traits, such as courage, honesty, and generosity, to be indications of a disposition to moderation, or the "golden mean." He observed that all praiseworthy actions are flanked by two extremes: courage by cowardice and rashness; honesty by deceit and bluntness; generosity by miserliness and profligacy (1980, pp. 45–46). He thus stands in contrast to the "black and white" thinking that has dominated Western ethics since the advent of Augustinian dualism.

Although Aristotle is the progenitor of character-based theory, not all character-based theorists share his belief in moderation as the source of all virtue. Phillipa Foot (1959), for example, states that moral character traits are simply part of the human composition, as are physical organs such as eyes and hands (p. 96). She claims that human beings could no more wish to lose virtues such as courage, honor, or honesty than they can wish to lose their arms or legs. She does not derive them from a basis in moderation but from a basis in human nature itself.

Character-based theories are popular among public administration scholars. A representative bibliography would include works by Stephen K. Bailey (1964), David K. Hart (1984, 1994), J. Patrick Dobel (1990, 1998), Terry L. Cooper (1987, 1991), Terry L. Cooper and N. Dale Wright (1992), and Kathryn G. Denhardt (1991, 1994). Thus, a body of literature is available that can provide the third point of the deontology–teleology–character triangle.

Character or virtue ethics begins with Aristotle's *Nichomachean Ethics,* the incunabulum or original sourcebook for a practical ethics of good character (Hart, 1994). A chief concern of virtue ethics is the obligation to transcend one's self-interest, to care for one's fellow citizens in community. One of the goals of the virtue ethics literature in public administration is the identification and definition of the characteristics or qualities of the virtuous administrator. For example, Bailey (1964) suggests that a recognition of moral ambiguity in people and policies, a recognition of the contexts conditioning moral priorities in the public service, and a recognition of the paradox of procedures constitute the three essential mental attitudes for public administrators, while the three essential moral qualities of the ethical public administrator are optimism, courage, and fairness tempered by charity. To Bailey, these attitudes and qualities, taken together, constitute a normative model for the public service and the hallmark of the morally mature public servant.

Hart (1984, 1994) argues that there is a moral link between the virtuous citizen and the honorable bureaucrat and that virtue ethics emphasizes the development of internal qualities of character, rather than obedience to moral rules. Furthermore, to achieve virtuous citizenship, Hart suggests four requirements: (1) doing moral philosophy, which means that the primary and permanent responsibility of a virtuous citizen is to ascertain the truth about the moral nature of individuals, to assimilate that truth to oneself, and to cast it in terms of one's civic life; (2) belief, which means that the virtuous citizen must believe that American regime values are true; (3) individual moral responsibility, which means that the virtuous citizen must act as an independent and responsible moral agent, who can never tolerate the instrumental use of any person nor acquiesce in her or his own instrumental use; and (4) civility, which means courtesy, respect, consideration, and most important, forbearance and tolerance. Forbearance is essential for minimizing public rules, and tolerance is not indifference but, rather, an amalgam of passion and intellect.

Hart (1984) also maintains that bureaucrats carry a dual status. Their fundamental obligation, like that of all citizens, is to seek virtue, and their professional obligations must be built from that foundation. "A democracy dependent upon virtuous citizens requires honorable bureaucrats" (p. 116). Moreover, the public administrator becomes the honorable bureaucrat through the possession of superior prudence, which, citing Adam Smith, Hart suggests consists of wise and judicious conduct directed to nobler purposes than individual fortune or reputation. Finally, to cultivate superior prudence, the public administrator must assume four duties: (1) moral significance; (2) caring; (3) moral entrepreneurism; and (4) noblesse oblige. With respect to moral significance, Hart argues that essential to determining what is morally significant is a complete understanding of and commitment to American regime values. When confronted with an unjust policy, the honorable bureaucrat, rather than resign—which Hart contends would be an abdication of responsibility to regime values—must refuse to comply and, indeed, become a moral hero if such action does not correct the situation. Caring involves having the best interests of citizens at heart, while moral entrepreneurism involves a willingness to take a moral risk and to assume the trustworthiness of citizens. The last duty, noblesse oblige, means moral nobility, the notion that the more one benefits from society, the more one is obliged to reciprocate.

Hart (1994) discusses virtue ethics in six categories: (1) cardinal virtues; (2) moral excellence; (3) moral action; (4) moral intentionality and voluntarism; (5) moral reinforcement and refreshment; and (6) living the best life. In regard to cardinal virtues—which historically consisted of prudence, justice, fortitude, temperance, and, later, faith, hope, and charity—Hart simplifies the list by reducing the cardinal virtues to two: eudaimonism and benevolence. He believes that eudaimonism—the condition of living in harmony with one's innate potentiality or living in truth to oneself—is the first cardinal virtue, and that benevolence—the love of others—is its equal. Neither is derivable from the other, and the other virtues can be derived from them. Hart concludes that we are all born with an innate imperative to virtue, that virtue is necessary to be fully human, that cardinal virtues must be intentionally cultivated, that they must emerge in intentional, voluntary moral action, and that they require endless moral improvement.

Dobel (1990) argues that the "ideal of personal integrity describes a condition where individuals can hold multiple realms of judgment in tension while keeping some coherence in their actions and lives" (p. 355). Personal integrity, according to Dobel, provides a framework for understanding how "individuals can simultaneously hold several commitments and balance among them in a morally defensible manner" (p. 355). Further, personal integrity "arises from people's ability to create a moral unity by organizing their activities and roles around central commitments which they view as centering their selfhood" (p. 355), and "[p]eople of integrity can give persuasive and plausible accounts of how the various dimensions of their lives fit together in manners consistent with their most basic commitments" (p. 356). Our ability to meet legal, official, or professional expectations rests in our personal capacity for integrity.

With reference to public administrators in particular, Dobel (1990) offers seven commitments that should frame the exercise of public integrity: (1) Be truthfully accountable to relevant authorities and publics; (2) address the public values of the regime; (3) respect and build institutions and procedures to achieve goals; (4) ensure fair and adequate participation of the relevant stakeholders; (5) seek competent performance in the execution of policy and program; (6) work for efficiency in the operation of government; (7) connect policy and program with the self-interest of the public and participants in such a way that the basic purposes are not subverted. In Dobel's view, these seven commitments connect and reinforce the three realms that comprise the aspects of public integrity: regime accountability, personal responsibility, and prudence. He recognizes, however, that in the end, "public integrity should be conceived of not in rigid and closed terms, but as dynamic and accountable. All public discretion is exercised by real human beings and made possible by personal integrity" (p. 364).

In a discussion of prudence and leadership, Dobel (1998) notes that recent theorists have argued that a virtue-based ethics focuses on the moral quality of the person and can inform an ethics of leadership. The ethics of prudence focuses on the obligation of a leader to achieve moral self-mastery, to attend to the context of a situation, and to seek concrete outcomes that are legitimate and durable. According to Dobel, while prudence is a necessary but not sufficient condition for ethical leadership, theorists since Aristotle have argued that, of all the virtues, it is the linchpin of political judgment.

Leadership entails ethics because leaders have responsibilities, the first of which is self-mastery. "All virtues and the personal capacity to live up to promises, obey the law, and follow directives depend upon this primary moral capacity" (p. 75). People in positions of responsibility are obligated to control their passions and overcome temptations; they must possess self-discipline. Self-command makes moral life possible; self-mastery lays the groundwork for ethical leadership. Virtue ethics extends self-mastery to the way people should develop their character and patterns of reaction and engagement with life. A virtue embodies a pattern of habitual perception and behavior, which arises from rearing, training, and self-development. To possess a virtue means a person's emotions and perceptions are aligned with moral purposes and support responsible judgment. In public life, virtues do not replace laws, norms, or duties, but they give life to these moral imperatives. In complicated, morally ambiguous situations, "virtues provide the stability of judgment and endurance to pursue moral commitment across time and obstacles" (p. 75). Yet, virtues require judgment in their exercise. Virtues may conflict with other virtues, like principles, or they may be subsumed by other less-desirable ends, such as the soldier who acts with courage but serves an evil cause. Virtues cannot provide the moral foundations of all action. They coexist in dialogue with norms, principles, and conceptions of the good society.

Cooper (1987) contends that a complete normative ethic for public administration must include an understanding of appropriate ethical principles, identification of virtues supportive of those principles, and analytical techniques to be used in specific situations to interpret the principles. The problem, however, is that managers responsible for the well-being of organizations seem to allow organizational status, position, and power to prevail over subordinates' professional ethics. In an effort to understand why, Cooper suggests the concept of practices and virtues developed by Alasdair MacIntyre as a useful perspective. Cooper also cites the work of other scholars—including Stuart Hampshire, James Wallace, R. E. Ewin, and William Frankena—as part of the revival of interest in virtue. All see virtues as inclinations or dispositions to act, not just to think or feel in a certain way. Virtues are traits of character, more or less reliable, tendencies to conduct oneself in a generally consistent fashion under similar conditions. They are not innate, however. They must be cultivated, which means, according to these scholars, that virtues involve cognitive activity, not conditioned, reflex behavior. Reason is used in addressing particular situations, with a certain established attitude and a conditioned will.

In a volume on citizenship in public administration, Cooper (1991) devotes a chapter to the public administrator as virtuous citizen. In his view, the critical trait of ethical citizenship is civic virtue, defined as "self-interest rightly understood," by which the citizen administrator acts to support the common good (p. 169). Moreover, civic virtue, according to Cooper, is "the central character trait necessary for the legitimate practice of public administration in a democratic society," and "requires support by three other subordinate virtues: public spiritedness, prudence, and substantive rationality" (pp. 169–170). Here, Cooper and Dobel diverge on the level of importance accorded to prudence. Finally, a year later, Cooper and Wright edited *Exemplary Public Administrators: Character and Leadership in Government* (Cooper and Wright, 1992), which contains discussions by Cooper and Hart on virtue and moral exemplars, respectively, followed by eleven essays on public servants who exemplify virtue in both their personal and professional lives. The book concludes with Cooper's reflections on exemplars of virtue.

To Denhardt (1991), the moral core of public administration consists of honor, benevolence, and justice. Honor "is the preeminent virtue in that it is understood as magnanimity or greatmindedness, presupposing excellence in all of the virtues. Honor denotes a quality of character in which the individual exhibits a high sense of duty, pursuing good deeds as ends in themselves, not because of any benefit or recognition that might be accrued because of the deeds" (p. 103). Benevolence "requires not just doing good but also a driving motivation to do good *for the sake of others*" (p. 104). This contrasts with beneficence or performing acts of kindness and charity, which "is a somewhat lower standard in that the acts need only be kind and charitable, but no such motivation or concern is demanded of the individual responsible for the act" (p. 104). Finally, justice, which "signifies fairness and regard for the rights of others," "can only be ensured through the virtuous acts of public servants *and* through a set of laws and other institutions that protect the rights of individuals" (pp. 106–107).

Denhardt (1994) believes that "character ethics has the power to transform public administration, and transform governance as we know it" (p. 2165). Character ethics requires perceptiveness, discernment, and a predisposition to judge and act with courage. Character ethics also would allow the public their rightful role in self-governance. "But if an ethic of character is to take hold in public administration, we need to design organizational environments and management practices more conducive to the development of virtuous habits" (p. 2165). Unfortunately, public institutions and the constraints on public servants have furthered moral illiteracy more than virtuous character. "In the name of efficiency, effectiveness, impartiality, and professionalism, public administration has moved along a path that has valued expert technical analysis more than moral dialogue among affected parties, and impartiality more than care or compassion" (pp. 2167–2168). At the same time, according to Denhardt, our workplaces do not foster productivity, creativity, effectiveness, or satisfaction. Therefore, we focus on movements such as Total Quality Management (TQM), which requires empowerment, not control. In Denhardt's view, even though "TQM and similar management reforms might be adopted for the sake of productivity and quality improvement, they might also present an opportunity to create a workplace considerably more conducive to the development and expression of virtuous character" (p. 2181). She is hopeful that, at least in theory, more participatory workplaces could lead to organizational transformation, an environment in which "the development of character and the expression of virtue could flourish" (p. 2181). On the other hand, prospects for such transformation are mixed. Denhardt suggests that some public administrators are up to the task, having demonstrated character and competence in their judgments, while others "have become so morally illiterate that it will take considerable time and experience for them to reestablish the capacity to exercise judgment of this kind" (p. 2182). Time and training will tell.

Character-based theorists share a common problem. They must explain why their favored character traits are considered morally good. While Aristotle, for example, considers those who are disposed to act in accordance with the mean to be good, he still must answer the question, "Why is that disposition good?" In the case of Foot, we may ask a similar question, although it should be framed differently because of the specifics of her theory. She mentions that traits such as courage and honesty are not things of which we can reasonably choose to be deprived. But there are also other, nonmoral traits and characteristics of which we cannot choose to be deprived. One cannot reasonably choose to be deprived of intelligence, assertiveness, or a sense of humor, but those traits are not generally considered moral. She must explain why some traits that we would not be without are in a separate moral class. More generally, character-based theorists must explain why their favored character traits are of moral significance.

We may also ask this question of any moral traits: "Why are they good while others are bad?" For example, why is honesty a good trait while selfishness, also a natural human characteristic, is a vice? This problem extends to the public administration theorists that we examined. For example, Hart's cardinal virtues of eudaimonism and benevolence may be generally considered good things, but one might ask why they are good. Likewise, Cooper (1991) considers "self-interest rightly understood" to be the critical trait of ethical citizenship, but why is self-interest, even in its most enlightened form, a moral good? Earlier, we saw that Frederickson merely declared that equality is a moral virtue without explaining why. The same problem exists here. This is not to say that we reject the various favored character traits. We agree that they are indeed virtues. But it is not enough merely to declare a virtue to be a good thing. One must provide an explanation concerning why it is good.

In the complexity of Aristotle's theory, such an explanation may be found. For Aristotle, moral behavior has two aspects, one of which is in the best interest of the agent of moral action but the other of which is in the interests of the society (1980, p. 2). He considers the ethical person to be the ultimately happy person, and, in Aristotle's optimistically unified view of nature, to be of ultimate benefit to the society in which he or she lives. For example, the courageous person is happier, by virtue of his courage, than the coward and also better than the coward with respect to the welfare and advancement of the social order. Such an explanation may be implicit also in Cooper's enlightened self-interest, Hart's eudaimonism and benevolence, and Denhardt's belief in the power of character to transform public administration and governance.

We need not accept entirely Aristotle's reasoning in order to learn from it. Despite his status as the font of character-based theories, he embeds his own character-based theory in a teleological context. His virtues are not merely good for an arbitrary reason or for no reason at all. They function to benefit both the individual and the society in which he or she lives. The relation between moral virtue in most circumstances and teleological considerations is evident. In Aristotle's ingenious propensity to unify theories, he combines teleology and character-based theories into a coherent whole. However, his comprehensive analysis leaves us with two questions: First, which of the two—character traits or teleology—is the ultimate justification for moral behavior? Second, if teleology can be combined with character-based theory, why can deontology, intuitionism, and perhaps even other theories of ethics not also be combined into a more comprehensive whole? Those questions form the basis of the issue to be discussed in the following chapter.

4

The Unification of Ethical Theories

Chapter 3 established that absolutist theories, unlike relativistic theories, could be used as guides to ethical behavior. However, all of the absolutist theories were problematic and seemed in conflict with each other. In this chapter, we remove those difficulties and unify the theories into a comprehensive whole. Our unification may alter the theories as they were expressed in chapter 3 and may also present them in ways that their authors did not anticipate or even approve. However, we do not consider agreement with the authors nearly as important as their insights, although perhaps in a slightly different form from that originally intended. For example, if a valuable truth can be extracted from Kant's theory, it is not of ultimate importance that Kant, himself, noticed that truth.

We begin with the generally accepted distinction between teleological and deontological theories. Those who insist on maintaining a rigid separation of the two are faced with a serious problem: They would require that advocates of each of the theories deprive obviously moral actions of any moral value. The deontologist, for example, would have to dismiss an act as morally empty if it was motivated solely by concern for the consequences. If President Lincoln, in signing the Emancipation

Proclamation, acted out of concern for the slaves that he would free rather than out of a principle such as "All people are equal," the deontologist would deny the act its moral value. Likewise, if Lincoln's sole concern were obedience to the principle that people should not be enslaved, the teleologist would be required to dismiss the moral nature of the act because of its disregard for consequence. The acts that one of the ethical classifications would deem saintly would be amoral to the other. Yet, any reasonable and unbiased assessment of each of the acts would find it morally praiseworthy.

Let us consider also those who, at great risk, protected Jewish residents of Nazi Germany from persecution. If the actions of those benefactors were based upon principle, with no concern for ultimate consequence, ethical teleology would deem them morally misguided. On the other hand, if the benefactors thought only of the consequence, while paying no mind to principle, ethical deontology would dismiss them as morally bereft.

The teleological and deontological aspects of moral actions are so interconnected that separating them becomes pointless and futile. Was Lincoln acting on the basis of principle or consequences? The question presents a false dichotomy. The principle of equality and the consequence of accelerating the process of emancipation are part and parcel of each other. The deontological principle that all people should be free would be worthless if there were no desired consequences to allowing people their freedom. If no one had wanted freedom or any benefits that follow from it, no one would ever have asserted a natural or constitutional right to be free. Such an assertion would have made no more sense than a claim of a natural right to drink sea water.

The artificiality of the distinction between deontology and teleology is unfortunately supported by the leading philosophers of both traditions. Kant (1989) claims that a truly good moral action is performed without any satisfaction or enjoyment, but strictly out of duty. He disclaims all benevolent and altruistic feelings as morally insignificant, regardless of their effects, because a true moral act is dispassionate.

Bentham (1970), by contrast, claims that there are no inherently moral motives, no matter how noble they are, but only good consequences. Motives are good, not in themselves, but only because of their tendency to promote happiness.

Such extreme comments belie the nearly universal human judgments that the moral philosophers themselves seek to justify. Consider an act done purely out of duty. It is admirable, but only in a limited way. Now consider that same act performed with the same degree of obedience to duty but accompanied also by a love of humanity strong enough itself to motivate the act. Kant may be correct in concluding that a moral act can be performed out of duty alone, but the act would be better yet if it displayed characteristics of a benevolent human being rather than a dispassionate moral machine.

In response to Bentham, one might provide a mirror-image counter-example. First, we may consider an act performed out of an enlightened self-interest that inevitably results in happiness for all. For example, a megalomaniacal public benefactor who craves public approval may give large sums of money to secure self-satisfaction. While Kant's rejection of such an act as devoid of moral content may be harsh, the act would nevertheless be more morally praiseworthy if combined with a recognition of a duty, which itself would produce the same welcome results. The utilitarian Bentham appears, like the deontologist Kant, to have explored one aspect of morality to the exclusion of any other, while the inclusion of both would have provided a richer account.

Unification of Teleology and Deontology

Rather than two distinct categories, teleology and deontology are interwoven into a single moral complex. But if so, there must be a rational structure by which they are unified. There are two possible ways in which they can be conceptually united. They may be distinct parts of a composite whole, such as the two wings of a butterfly or two pieces of a jigsaw puzzle; or they may be united as different yet consistent ways of describing the same thing, as are "red" and "the shortest light waves in the visible spectrum." We favor the second option because it seems more consistent with examples such as the case of Lincoln's signing of the Proclamation.

Under the first option, teleology and deontology are two distinct portions of an ethical whole. William Frankena (1963) attempts to construct such a theory by reducing all ethics to two principles: a principle of benevolence, which requires us to produce good consequences and prevent harmful ones; and a principle of justice that requires that we treat people equally (pp. 37–38). But Frankena leaves some questions unanswered. First, why are there not other principles, such as "Do not lie" or "Treat sentient beings as more valuable than inanimate objects." The choice of two seems arbitrary. Second, although he claims to combine teleology and deontology, his analysis is, in the end, teleological. He argues that "Morality was made for man, not man for morality" and thus suggests that the whole moral endeavor has human benefit as its *telos* (p. 37).

A third problem with Frankena's theory—or any theory that purports to divide morality into separate segments—is its implicit distinctness of the teleological and deontological parts. As the example of Lincoln suggests, they are intimately interconnected. He did not have two distinct moral motives or reasons, one teleological and the other deontological; they were indistinguishable. He did not perform distinct teleological and deontological moral acts; he acted teleologically in acting deontologically.

Aristotle, in unifying conceptual, Platonic form and atomistic matter, argued that all objects have both in an inseparable unity and can no more be separated than a piece of bronze and its shape (1956, p. 125). Similarly, we propose, the deontological and the teleological are unified in the moral decision as aspects of a complex ethical whole. Likewise, one might argue that a lightning bolt is the same thing as a flow of electronic particles, although both descriptions are of a different order (Smart, 1971, p. 58). It would be pointless to insist that lightning is really not a bolt of light in the sky but rather a movement of unperceivable particles, and it would be equally pointless to insist the reverse. The description that is more appropriate depends upon the context and upon one's purposes. So also with a color and its corresponding wavelength. For scientific purposes, the wavelength description would be preferable, but it would not be very useful for aesthetic purposes such as teaching an art student about color relations.

In a similar manner, modern theorists of mind often argue that mind and brain are an inseparable unity (Place, 1966). They argue that when one feels pain, there are not two events—one in the brain and the other in the incorporeal mind—but one event that can be described either as a brain state or as a subjective experience. Thus, it may be maintained that any mental event is, at the same time, a neurological or brain event. However, one should not therefore conclude that it is possible to describe such experiences equally well under either conceptual structure. In different cases, one or the other might provide a clearer explanation. When explaining sudden irrational mood swings, the neurological explanation would likely be more helpful. But the individual's own report of his "inner" mind's activities would be much more helpful in his explanation of how he solved a mathematics problem. The mental and physical descriptions are complementary rather than mutually exclusive.

If our analogy applies, it can explain important aspects of the relation of teleology and deontology. In many cases, the same moral action can be equally satisfactorily explained using either ethical approach. The case of Lincoln's signing of the Emancipation Proclamation would be one such instance; it could easily be justified on grounds of either the best interest of society or deontological justice. Yet, as with descriptions of the mind, there may be some cases in which one means of analysis works better. Teleological explanations might explain more lucidly the case in which the head of state must lie to protect national security, and deontological explanations may more clearly show why the thinning out of the human herd is undesirable. Even in such cases, however, we hold that an ultimate reconciliation exists but is not immediately evident, as one might suppose that, someday, subjective and neurological descriptions of the mind may be rendered utterly interchangeable. Later in this chapter, we attempt to make progress in this reconciliation.

The apparent confusion that we found, expressed either explicitly or implicitly, in the writings of public administration theorists such as Stewart, Denhardt, and Frederickson is therefore understandable. The confusion is not so much in the public administration practices that they observe or in their theories as in the deontological–teleological distinction itself.

One might advance an objection to our unification of teleology and deontology by asking whether a person can act deontologically but not teleologically, or *vice versa*. This request presents an apparent problem for our position because we have argued that teleology and deontology are, at a deep level, identical, as are red and the wavelength of red. Everything that is red shares that wavelength and every emanation of light of that wavelength is red. It would seem to follow, then, that every teleological act must also be deontological and every deontological act must also be teleological. However, Kant is often interpreted as favoring actions that are deontological but not teleological, while Mill is often interpreted as favoring acts that eschew deontological considerations in favor of teleological. If our position is correct, no such distinction should be possible.

In response, let us point out that people rarely consider their actions exclusively deontological or teleological. Most moral acts are performed without a view to theoretical purity and are, like that in the Lincoln example, characterized equally by teleological and deontological aspects. However, even the rare case must be explained. To understand it, we must examine the color–wavelength analogy more closely.

While all things that are red emit the same wavelength, it is possible to be aware of a red object under one description but not the other. Few people have the vaguest idea of the wavelength of the light shining off a rose but are very much aware of its beautiful hue. By contrast, a color-blind physicist may have remarkable knowledge of the red shift and other matters relating to the wavelength of light without ever having perceived any color at all. Color and wavelength may be identical, but their identity may be hidden to those who know only one aspect of the phenomenon. Similarly, we maintain, when one performs a correct teleological act, she also performs a correct deontological act, although she may be unaware of its deontological nature; and when one performs a correct deontological act, she also performs a correct teleological act, although she may be unaware of its teleological nature.

Herein lies the source of the mutual misunderstanding between teleologists and deontologists. Each is like an artist mixing colors to produce a particular shade of red without knowing that he is producing a specific wavelength. If a physicist informed him of the scientific aspects of the color, the artist may protest that he is creating nothing so sterile and mathematical as a light wave but a beautiful visual object. Such an artist would fail to understand that the scientific explanation does not conflict with his own but only describes the same thing from a different aspect. The Kantian considers only the strictly rational aspect of the moral act, whereas the utilitarian considers only the consequences; and each complains that the other's seemingly conflicting accounts must be false. But if they examined their own reasoning more fully and understood ethics more comprehensively, they would discover no ultimate disagreement.

Teleology in Kantianism

Kant has long been considered as a caricature of the deontologist so rigid as to disregard as morally insignificant any concern for consequence. Some of his own remarks, scattered throughout the corpus of his work, support such a stern interpretation. However, some of his other comments suggest that Kant need not be read so rigidly, as Roger Sullivan (1991), Thomas Auxter (1982), and Marcia Baron (1995), among others, argue. If, as we have maintained, teleology and deontology cannot be neatly separated, Kant's deontology must have teleological aspects. But we should avoid an inordinate concern with the matter of exactly what Kant, himself, intended in every nuance of his theory. The job of inferring what was in Kant's mind as he wrote his ethical and political treatises is an interesting scholarly enterprise but is a secondary matter to those concerned more with proper behavior than with the history of ideas. We examine Kant more for the insights that his theory contains than for an accurate reconstruction of his personal beliefs

Kant attempted to derive ethics from reason. The first law of reason is the admonition against self-contradiction, which, although self-evident conceptually, has never been formulated in uncontested language. Since even logicians cannot agree on the wording of the admonition, Kant cannot be expected to specify it perfectly in ethics, a far more complex subject than formal logic. He offers three attempts to state his categorical imperative, but he regards none as flawless. Even the claim that there are only three formulations is misleading. In *Fundamental Principles of the Metaphysics of Morals* (1989) he changes the wording of each formulation nearly every time he presents it. Nevertheless, the formulations can be subsumed under three general statements: Always act according to a maxim that you could will to be a universal law; treat all rational beings as ends in themselves and not as means; respect the autonomy of rational beings to produce a "kingdom of ends" (i.e., ethical world) (p. 48). The formulations are not different principles but different attempts to put the concept of rational consistency into words. None of the formulations is complete in itself.

We believe that too much attention has been paid to the formulations and not enough to the intent of Kant's categorical imperative. Understandably, Kant attempted to provide the clearest formulation possible, but the essential Kantian message is not undermined by his inability to provide an exact statement. The inability of logicians, epistemologists, and metaphysicians to formulate the concept of consistency does not require abandonment of the concept. Just as it is often impossible to translate statements perfectly from one language to another, it is not always possible to translate concepts into language, in general. Our interpretation of Kant will focus on the message of consistency and rationality in behavior rather than on the problems of linguistic expression. We will regard Kant's formulations as strong though imperfect guidelines directing people to rational action.

The unrealistic expectation that Kant should provide a clear and unambiguous formula to apply to all cases lends credibility to a common criticism. Because he provides no such formula, his critics often suppose that his theory cannot be applied at all. However, an emphasis on the intent of his formulations rather than their literal statement permits application more fully that any statement could.

We have already considered an example of the undue emphasis upon formulation rather than intent. Kant's second formulation states that one should never treat another rational being as a means but only as an end. A literal, narrow interpretation of that formulation would preclude hiring someone to perform a service, because to use someone's skill and labor is to treat that person as a means. However, a more reasonable interpretation would emphasize the intent of the action. To hire someone with the full intent of providing due compensation, even if the employee requests less than is deserved, would demonstrate the intent of treating someone as an end in itself. In this case, the literal interpretation of the formulation is clearly not as appropriate as its intent.

Overemphasis on formulation rather than intent is also the source of another frequent criticism of Kant: His theory constantly results in unresolvable conflicts between equally supportable moral rules. In his famous example, Jean-Paul Sartre (1947) argues that Kant is unable to assist a young man torn between fighting in the Resistance and caring for his aging, needy mother. Sartre claims that Kant is not helpful because either alternative entails using one party to aid the other. However, Sartre overlooks the intent of the young man as well as the intent of the formulations of the categorical imperative. In no case does the young man display any intent to use his mother for the sake of the Resistance or the Resistance for the sake of his mother. If he did, he would not have been so earnest in his discussion with Sartre. Further-more, we maintain that a solution to the young man's problem can be inferred from Kant. To care for one's mother is, in most cases, a natural human inclination derived from a private relationship. Such activity, humane and laudable as it is, is based upon emotional more than rational factors. Such activity is directed at a person *qua* mother rather than rational being. If the activity were directed at the person, *qua* rational being, it would be directed at all people rather than specifically at one's mother. On the other hand, the Nazis represented, as clearly as possible, use of human beings as means. To oppose them, with the intent of saving human beings, as such, from repression, would express the intrinsic value of human beings rather than as mothers, fathers, children, or in any other roles or personal relationships.

Roger Sullivan (1991) gives further support to a more flexible inter-pretation of Kant. Sullivan points out that, while Kant considers it a moral obligation to follow the moral rule that properly applies to a situation, there is no formula to determine when a rule applies or which of two possible rules applies to the situation.

> Now imagine a person who seems morally obligated to perform two different actions simultaneously by the same moral rule to keep his word. He has promised to meet another person, fully intending to do so, but finds out, just before the appointed time, that he needs to take his wife to the hospital. Unless there are other morally contravening considerations, clearly he is entitled to judge that his *sole* duty *at that moment* is to take care of his wife (p. 74).

Sullivan adds that such a case is not an exception to the rule requiring promise keeping but that, in this case, there is no obligation to keep the promise.

It is obvious that the rule "Do not lie" properly applies when one is contemplating lying, for purely selfish reasons, to an innocent customer for the purpose of inducing him to buy a product for an inflated price. But it is unclear whether that rule should apply to a head of state who must, for the purposes of preserving the secrecy of negotiations that could avoid a war, deny that they even exist. The intent of "Do not lie" clearly applies unambiguously in the first case, but in the second, one might say that a rule such as "A head of state must avoid war whenever possible" is the truly applicable rule. One could imagine the foolish extremes of telling a host that her *coq au vin*, over which she slaved for hours, was a disappointment, against all common courtesy; telling a hospitalized person who needs encouragement that he appears corpse-like; never telling a joke for fear that the story will momentarily be believed until the punch line is uttered. As Sullivan suggests, these are not exceptions to the rule against lying but cases in which the rule is inapplicable (p. 74).

Determining which rule is applicable in a particular case is a matter of judgment. No rule can fully contain another rule telling us when to apply it. In some cases, such as that of Sartre's confused young man, the determination of the properly applied rule may not be obvious, leaving considerable room for disagreement. However, for Kant, the intent of the categorical imperative, as expressed in his three formulations, must guide judgment.

Kant, as we interpret him, can be applied to public administration at both a theoretical and a practical level. At the theoretical level, the intent of Kant's second formulation of the categorical imperative provides for ethical autonomy for public administrators. Recognition of each individual as a rational, autonomous, intrinsically valuable being requires that people be treated as independent decision makers rather than as formula-driven mechanisms. A system that prevents any-one—especially a person hired for his or her expertise—from using free rational judgment is not only ineffective but, under Kantian analysis, unethical. However, the autonomy is not license for any decisions or actions that the practitioner might take. Just as the practitioner's autonomy has its roots in ethical theory, he or she must exercise it in an ethical manner. Kantian consistency requires that autonomy not be used to undermine its own *raison d'etre*. The autonomy that Kant grants is the freedom to behave responsibly and ethically, not a freedom from ethics.

Kant's theory also provides a context for the analysis, interpretation, and implementation of principal–agent relations, moral leadership, and a host of organizational processes such as planning and budgeting, program evaluation, and performance appraisal. While public administrators are autonomous, they must treat with respect all others, including the public that charges them, the beneficiaries of services, and professional colleagues. For example, to use discretionary funds to advance the personal interests of the members of the organization would be to treat the public as a means rather than an end. To sacrifice the quality of service to increase the number of people served and, thus, to increase funding is to treat both the public and the served individuals as means. To give inaccurate evaluations of subordinates is to use one's colleagues, to whom the evaluations are reported, as means.

Another issue may further demonstrate Kant's position: A matter of current concern among public administrators is privatization. There are plausible arguments both for and against this practice. Public administrators also may have a self-interest in removing the threat of privatization, but that self-interest should not be the basis for their opposition. If privatization serves the people better, to oppose it would be to use the public as a means to one's own self-interest. Such an abuse is probably unnecessary in the vast majority of cases, because there is no clear evidence that privatization is beneficial. Yet, cases arise in which the public is strongly tempted to opt for privatization. In such cases, Kant would argue, any opposition to privatization should be based upon the interest of the public rather than the interests of public employees.

But let us suppose that the public, lacking the experience of the administrator and unaware of the effects of privatization on accountability, responsiveness, and organizational morale, cannot be convinced on rational grounds that privatization is unwise. Perhaps a public administrator strongly believes but cannot rationally prove to an elected body, such as a city council, that privatization would damage the public interest. Should the manager present a more effective, although some-what deceptive case based more on rhetoric than reason? Charles Fox (1989) discusses such a hypothetical instance in "Free to Choose, Free to Win, Free to Lose: The Phenomenology of Ethical Space":

> Furthermore, if some deception has occurred it has been, after all based on real facts, however arranged on the basis of what the manager firmly believes is inductively derived from valid hypotheses. Moreover, how can she mention employee morale to a council of small business-men who ignore their own employees' attitudes? (p. 927).

Fox argues that, in such a case, a deceptive argument is acceptable.

A Kantian respect for persons as rational ends in themselves would allow no semblance of deception, even in the stated circumstances. The administrator in the example assumes that the audience is not fully rational. Because of her use of deception, the council members' auton-omy is not fully respected, and they are being treated as means to an albeit laudable end. Furthermore, the administrator is inconsistent. While denying that her position as director of a threatened agency clouds her judgment, she presupposes that the council members must be biased because they are businessmen.

The above examples suggest another common complaint against Kant. His theory is often criticized as too demanding to be followed in all or even nearly all cases. This criticism, however, is unjustified when one understands that any moral theory must, by its nature, be demand-ing. We can accept as axiomatic the proposition that no person or system is perfect. Any ethical theory that rendered perfection attainable would be justly criticized as uninspiring and mundane.

On the contrary, the demanding, idealistic nature of Kant's theory provides a vision. Like Plato's ideal, Kant's can function as a motivation for societal improvement. It need not be an immediate transformation to a perfect state but, instead, could be incremental, as is the progress of history generally. Without such an ideal to define and measure progress, it is less likely to occur. We do not maintain that our interpretation of Kant will unambiguously resolve all of the ethical problems that public administrators encounter. However, our analysis refutes critics who claim that Kant's theory is essentially inapplicable to most practical cases.

The often unnoticed flexibility in Kant's theory permits his reconciliation with teleology. Sullivan (1991) suggests such a reconciliation in several ways. First, he points out that, in both *Critique of Practical Reason* (1949) and the *Metaphysics of Morals* (1991) Kant states explicitly that human behavior is, in its very nature, purposive (Sullivan, 1991, p. 184; Kant, 1949, p. 215; Kant, 1991, p. 277). More importantly, Sullivan notes that, for Kant, reason can itself establish objective moral ends (Sullivan 1991, p. 28). Among them are the development of virtuous character, the rational being as end in itself, and the establishment of the kingdom of ends. The latter two are clearly implicit in the second and third formulations of the categorical imperative. The recognition of the need to develop good character is implicit in the entire moral enterprise. Furthermore, Kant begins his analysis with the statement that a good will, which defines good character, is the only thing that is good without qualification. It follows that developing good character is a proper moral goal.

Thomas Auxter (1982) devotes his book, *Kant's Moral Teleology*, to dispelling the notion that Kant's deontology, far from excluding teleological considerations, requires them. He notes that "[a] right action must be in accordance with an acceptable, universalized maxim. A maxim is acceptable only if everyone can will it. But it makes no sense to ask whether everyone can will it unless we look at the consequences of willing the practice" (p. 3). To elaborate on this point, he notes that the first formulation of the categorical imperative is, at a literal level, a law about nothing unless it is assumed that the law is to be applied to purposive behavior (p. 63). He therefore implies that, if the first formulation is to make sense, it must presuppose a teleology in human action.

Later, in a passage expressing the Kantian ideal world, Auxter makes the following observation:

The ideal world is not an order where identical parts (human agents) simply add up (qua aggregate) to the whole. On the contrary, it is an order where each part contributes in its own way to the effect of the whole, which is a harmonious composition of the various contributions. . . . The moral realization of rational agents (the parts) is indeed the final purpose of the order, and it is because the whole functions effectively (as a result of the perfect functioning of the parts) that the individual rational agents (who do after all represent absolute value) can realize their moral purposes. . . . There are two ways that this happens in the ideal order. Because each member performs a social function, and because these functions cohere in a unified effect benefitting each member, we may say that each member contributes positively to the moral effectiveness of every other member. Secondly, because each member refrains from violating the rights of other members, each contributes to the kind of order in which every agent can follow the moral law freely and promote the purposes compatible with it (p. 70).

This quotation is significant for two reasons. First, it points out the teleological aspect of Kant's ideal world in which members "perform a social function" that coheres with other functions to "benefit each member." Second, the quotation exhibits the interweaving of teleology and deontology. Deontologically moral action necessarily produces a social good. Furthermore, part of that social good is the freedom to act according to the moral law. Moral action thus becomes both a means and an end, and social order becomes both an end and a means.

Marcia Baron (1995), making use of Kant's distinction between perfect and imperfect duties, further shows how teleology is fused with deontology in his ethical theory. Perfect duties "prescribe the actions that we are to take (or omit)." A duty such as "Do not lie," or "Do not steal," in which a specific act is described, is a perfect duty, most of which is expressed as a negation of actions. An imperfect duty, on the other hand, "prescribes 'only the maxim of the action . . . not the action itself' " (p. 30). An imperfect duty would be the duty to respect oneself;

one can fulfill this duty in numerous different ways by means of many actions. Among the Ten Commandments, "Do not murder" would be a perfect duty but "Honor thy parents" would be an imperfect duty.

Kant (1989) argues that we have imperfect duties to develop our talents and to contribute to the welfare of others in need (p. 40). He believes that, although it is within that range of logical possibility that one might will the complete loss of his or her talents and that one might adopt the rule that no one should help anyone, no sane person would will such things. Even out of self-interest, one would will one's own talents to be at least maintained and wish to live in a world in which she can depend upon others when they can easily help her in distress. Consequently, Kant infers that all rational, consistent human beings would accept self-development and service to the disadvantaged as imperfect duties. But Baron (1995) points out that they also define, as ends, one's own perfection and the happiness of others (p. 88). Here again, the teleological and deontological fuse in Kant.

A passage from Kant's *Metaphysics of Morals* (1991) exhibits this fusion, as Baron suggests, in the imperfect duty to promote happiness.

> The reason that it is a duty to be beneficent is this: Since our self love cannot be separated from our need to be loved (helped in the case of need) by others as well, we therefore make ourselves an end for others; and the only way this maxim is binding is through its qualification as a universal law, hence through our will to make others ends as well. The happiness of others is therefore an end that is also a duty (p. 197).

In light of the analyses of Sullivan, Auxter, and Baron, we can observe teleological implications in all three of Kant's formulations of the categorical imperative. The first, "Act according to a maxim that you could will to be a universal law," makes sense only under the assumption that one is acting, and thus behaving with an intent or purpose. That formulation becomes a regulating principle to apply to any action, regardless of its purpose, but under the supposition that it has a purpose. Furthermore, as Auxter (1982) points out, the formulation implicitly asks the person contemplating an action to consider the world that would result if all human beings performed that action (p. 3). Only then can one determine whether the act is consistent. Thus, full application of the first formulation is impossible without implicit reference to consequence.

The second formulation—namely, human beings as ends in themselves—makes more explicit reference to ends. Furthermore, one must ask what is implicit in treating human beings as ends in themselves. Surely Kant means more than merely to bring them into existence and sustain them. To fully treat them as ends in themselves implies taking their interests into full consideration; that is to say, their happiness should be an end. When so understood, Kant's second formulation of the categorical imperative sounds very much like the admonition of a teleological utilitarian.

The third formulation is equally explicit in its teleological implications: Act in the manner of a legislator of a kingdom of ends, a society in which all human ends are consistent with each other. This formulation makes reference to ends in two ways. First, it asks that one behave in a manner that takes the purposes of all other human beings into account. Second, the establishment of a kingdom of ends, the political ideal for Kant, becomes an end of its own. That kingdom, in which all people are able to pursue their ends without conflict with or interference from others, would hardly be distinguishable from the utilitarian ideal of a world in which happiness is maximized.

One might argue that there is still an important difference between the utilitarian's utopia and Kant's kingdom of ends. In the kingdom of ends, happiness is promoted as a means to a world in which all ends can be consistent with each other and all human beings are able to act in accordance with consistent principles. Thus, happiness exists for the sake of principle and consistency. With the utilitarian, the case seems to be reversed: Principles are followed for the sake of happiness. But even so, the difference between the deontological Kantian and the teleological utilitarian is not altogether clear. For Kant, in his kingdom of ends, the happiness of others is among the ends that a person must consider in articulating his or her principles. For the utilitarian, as we will see in the following discussion, behaving according to principles is an activity that constitutes a major part of happiness.

It may now be objected that we are making Kant into a utilitarian and utilitarians into Kantians. There is some truth to that charge. We maintain that, like a description of the color red as perceived and a mathematical description of the wavelength of red, deontology and teleology describe the same phenomenon. Nevertheless, the descriptions are of different kinds. We maintain, then, that deontologists and teleologists think that they describe different things but are really describing the same thing, human ethics, from different but complementary perspectives.

Deontology in Utilitarianism

On the surface, utilitarianism, the predominant form of teleology, is diametrically opposed to Kantian deontology. Yet, just as closer observation of Kant revealed a teleology, the deontology implicit in utilitarianism emerges in its subtlety. Although utilitarians themselves may not notice, deontological considerations characterize utilitarianism at both theoretical and practical levels.

In theory, utilitarianism denies the supremacy of moral rules, subjugating them to the goal of maximization of happiness. But in making happiness an ultimate goal, the utilitarian is, despite himself, advancing an ultimate rule: One ought to maximize happiness. Mill (1979) himself refers to that rule as "the principle of utility" (p. 3) and "greatest happiness principle" (p. 7). Is happiness, then, an end or the substantial factor in a moral rule? We argue that there is no difference between the two. To argue that happiness is *really* an end only or that it is *really* only the basis of the rule "One ought to maximize happiness" is to perpetuate the false dichotomy between teleology and deontology. There is no substantial difference between saying that maximization of happiness is the ultimate goal of moral action and saying that one ought to maximize happiness.

But one must also ask of the utilitarian why happiness is the legitimate end of moral action. To that request, Mill provides the answer that happiness is that which every human being desires. Mill's claim is a psychological one, such that the foundation of all human desires and the motive for all human behavior is the pursuit of happiness (p. 34). Defense of that claim requires a creative definition of happiness, but we will have more to say on that matter later. If we assume that the utilitarian claim is true, it explains why any arbitrarily chosen person, let us call him Adam, should value, above all other things, happiness for himself. If Adam believes that claim, he can also infer that all others value happiness as he does. But he cannot yet infer the utilitarian's claim that we ought to maximize happiness without an additional moral premise. Adam may well recognize his own desire for happiness and that of others but infer that he should seek his own happiness while disregarding anyone else. Only if Adam finds a moral reason why he should promote the happiness of others can he reach agreement with the utilitarian. Even if Adam were motivated by a benevolent desire to help others, he would still have at best a compelling tendency to promote human happiness, but no moral reason why he should. Such a desire is, as we have argued, a necessary condition of a completely moral act but not a sufficient reason why such an act is morally required. Any justification that requires that one has a duty to promote the happiness of others—even at the expense of his own—must rely on a deontological claim that altruistic action is inherently better than egoistic action. There are several possible reasons for that claim: that, in order to be logically consistent, he should do unto others as he would have them do unto him; that he should regard others as having intrinsic value; or that he has a responsibility to do his best to create a world in which happiness abounds. All three of those justifications are essentially Kantian.

It has often been noted that utilitarianism presupposes that all people are equal, and that one person's happiness is no more important than that of anyone else. The concept of maximizing happiness would make little sense if some people were to be regarded as "more equal than others." But here, again, one must ask how that equality can be justified. It seems unjustifiable under utilitarianism because utilitarianism presupposes equality. A theory cannot justify one of its own presuppositions without arguing in a circle. Again, the Kantian beliefs that people are ends in themselves and that consistency requires that all people be treated equally are evident even in the overt teleology of the utilitarian.

In addition to theoretical aspects of deontology implicit in utilitarianism, it also has an implicit practical deontology. By "practical deontology" we mean behavioral recommendations that are virtually identical to those that deontology would recommend. Earlier, we saw that rule utilitarianism was adopted to respond to the criticism that utilitarians would be too quick to break hallowed moral rules, such as "Do not murder," to promote happiness.

John Rawls (1955), before he adopted his current, more Kantian position, defended the rule utilitarian position as the best response to such criticism. He argued that it failed to distinguish a justification for a practice and justification for a particular action falling under that practice (p. 3). He also argued that, once a general practice has been shown to promote happiness, one should almost never make exceptions. He used the example of a justice system in which innocent people may be condemned if the condemnation, in some peculiar but conceivable way, promoted social happiness. He called such a practice "telishment." In the following passage, he refutes telishment on utilitarian grounds:

> Once one realizes that one is involved in setting up such an institution, one sees that the hazards are very great. For example, what check is there on the officials? How is one to tell whether or not their actions are authorized? How is one to limit the risks involved in allowing such systematic deception? How is one to avoid giving anything short of complete discretion to the authorities to telish anyone they like? In addition to these considerations, it is obvious that people will come to

have a very different attitude towards their penal system when telishment is adjoined to it. They will be uncertain as to whether a convict has been punished or telished. They will be uncertain as to whether or not they should feel sorry for him. They will wonder whether the same fate won't at any time fall on them. If one pictures how such an institution would actually work, and the enormous risks involved in it, it seems clear that it would serve no useful purpose. A utilitarian justification for this institution is most unlikely (pp. 11–12).

Rawls therefore concludes that a society that follows rules that generally produce happiness would be happier than a society in which people broke rules whenever doing so seemed to promote happiness. The behavior that he would therefore suggest would be virtually indistinguishable from that of a committed Kantian.

At one point, Rawls seems to promote behavior different from that of a Kantian. Rawls claims that in cases that are so unusual that no rule has ever been shown to apply successfully from a consequentialist standpoint, one must promote happiness without relying upon rules. Such cases may arise if human beings discover strange creatures on other planets or if genetic research enables us to affect human development in new ways. But even in consideration of such cases, Rawls does not vary much, if at all, from Kant in practice. As we have seen, Kant, interpreted in the flexible manner that we and others have suggested, would recognize cases in which no rule of perfect duty applied and thus rely on the imperfect duty to promote happiness.

R. M. Hare (1952), in defending utilitarianism, notes that, while moral rules are ultimately justified by happiness and cannot be considered infallible, they must be taken very seriously by the moral agent. While arguing that utilitarian considerations are the ultimate justifications for moral action, he notes that "decisions cannot be taught; only rules can be taught" (p. 75). He compares the learning of ethics to learning how to drive (p. 76). One can do neither without following rules, even if one does not always understand them or recognize their ultimate utility.

In a later article (1976) Hare moves even closer to deontology and refers to his position as a Kantian version of utilitarianism. Here, he argues that a good person's tendency to follow moral rules, which generally lead to happiness, should be so ingrained that he will obey them even if, on a particular occasion, happiness would be best served by breaking them. Hare argues such strong tendencies are, all things considered, conducive to social happiness. Even if, on a few isolated occasions, those tendencies lead to unfortunate results, having those tendencies and consistently acting on them ultimately produces more happiness than harm.

Thus, we see a practical deontology in the developed utilitarianism expressed by Rawls and Hare. We find it unsurprising that both eventually came to advocate deontology. As we have indicated, we do not consider the movement from teleology to deontology a radical change.

Teleology resembles deontology even more when the utilitarians' notion of happiness is examined. For Mill, happiness is more than merely the acquisition of material goods. He would consider such a concept of happiness to befit a lower animal more than a human being. Mill (1979) claims that the quality, as well as the quantity of happiness, is to be considered in any evaluation (p. 8). Quality cannot be measured but can be recognized by the well-developed, mature, and experienced person. The quality of happiness enjoyed by a person who can take satisfaction in his principled actions would clearly outweigh the happiness of the unprincipled. Moreover, Mill claims that a fully moral person would make virtue and duty not only means to happiness but a part of happiness itself (pp. 35–37). A miser comes to find happiness in money, in itself, as a result of his associating it with the material good that it can purchase; likewise, a fully moral person will find happiness in virtue and duty in themselves because of their association with productivity of happiness. In both cases, something comes to be associated with its common effects.

Richard Brandt (1983), a twentieth-century teleologist, elaborates on the happiness that one finds in activities characteristic of a Kantian:

I myself think that some element of experience or activity is pleasant if it makes the person, at that time, want to continue or repeat it, simply for itself and not for extraneous reasons. . . . But when we start surveying the various items that philosophers have called good, like . . . qualities of character like courage or fairmindedness, we need to ask whether all of these do not make life more pleasant, and whether we would be much interested in them if they didn't (p. 40).

Teleologists would argue that, despite these theoretical and practical commonalities with deontology, a fundamental difference remains. For the deontologist, happiness is not the aim of moral activity but the result of behavior that derives its morality from its principle rather than its consequence. For the teleologist, on the other hand, happiness is the aim and the determinant of moral behavior. However, we do not argue that morality is described in the same way from both perspectives. We argue, instead, that the two perspectives are, like red and its wavelength, different but ultimately compatible descriptions of the same entity. The similarities that appear on close inspection of deontology and teleology are evidence of that compatibility.

Character-Based Theories as Part of the Unity

If teleology and deontology are, as we argue, different aspects of a unified ethic, then any theory that is teleological is also deontological and any theory that is deontological is also teleological. Therefore, if character-based theories can be unified with either one, they are also unified with the other.

One of the oldest character-based theories is that expressed in Plato's *Republic* (1991), wherein Plato examines morality by studying the virtues of a human being. Plato's theory is also suggestive of Kantianism in that Plato's ideal human being is governed by his or her rational faculties and behaves in accordance with reason. But also like Kant, Plato's theory is implicitly teleological, because the good person, acting out of duty instilled by reason, will act in a manner that advances the happiness of society. The happiness to be attained is one that comprises virtue, much like that of the utilitarians we have discussed. This duty is evident in the parable of the cave and the function of moral punishment as discussed in the *Republic*, where teleology and deontology are fused into character theory (pp. 12–13, 195).

As we have already noted, Aristotle's character-based theory has a teleological aspect. He regards a moral act as one that displays a tendency toward moderation, but that tendency is socially desirable, as are his favored specific virtues, such as courage, temperance, generosity. The individual is to pursue those virtues, as a deontologist would, for their own sake, but his or her pursuit of them generally benefits the society as a whole. The case is similar to that in which people pursue sex for its own sake, but, as an inevitable consequence, intended or not, promote the continued existence of the human species. This confluence of virtue pursued for its own sake and the social good is not surprising in the light of Aristotle's overall philosophic perspective, in which ethics is understood as subsidiary to politics, which promotes the general good. The relation of Aristotle to the utilitarianism advanced by Rawls, Hare, and Brandt is also evident; all four recommend the following of a practice, seemingly as a final end, that has a beneficial social result. Here, again, teleology, deontology, and character theory are interwoven.

Philippa Foot (1959) is a contemporary character-based theorist who reflects the same interweaving. She argues that moral virtues, by their close relation to the nature of a human being, must be considered desirable and cannot be disavowed. She suggests that to wish not to be courageous, honest, or just is akin to wishing not to have functioning bodily parts such as hands or eyes (p. 96). Someone who wished to be relieved of any of those moral attributes or those physical characteristics would be considered abnormal. The moral characteristics are valued, as deontologists would value them, as inherent moral goods. But she adds that the reason for our valuing of them as we do is that they enable us, as individuals and as a society, to live well.

Alisdair MacIntyre (1981) is among the best known twentieth-century character-based theorists, and it is especially important that we discuss his position because it appears to be at odds with our own. In one important respect, he agrees with our position: He claims that in his theory moral virtue has a *telos*. Yet, he claims that his position is opposed to utilitarianism. Although it may be considered sufficient, for our purposes, that MacIntyre acknowledges his teleology, we argue, further, that he is closer to utilitarianism than he realizes.

His disagreement with utilitarianism is based upon his distinction between internal and external goods. His concept of an internal good is introduced in his rather long and difficult definition of a practice: "a coherent and complex form of socially cooperative human activity through which goods internal to that activity are realized in the course of trying to achieve those standards of excellence which are appropriate to, and partially definitive of, that form of activity with the result that human powers to achieve excellence, and human conceptions of the ends and goods involved, are systematically extended" (p. 175). He states later that an internal good can be specified only as existing within a practice and can be recognized only by the experience of participating in the practice. For example, if a child is induced with the lure of candy to learn to play chess, the candy is an external good that the child recognizes. The internal good that he must achieve to secure his reward is excellence, or at least the best semblance of it that a novice can provide, in the skills that lead to success in chess.

MacIntyre argues that, while societies recognize different character states as virtues, they share something in common. They are regarded as virtues because they function within the practices of those societies (pp. 180–181). The practices themselves bring the individuals into relationships with other members of the society, including those of the past and those yet unborn. Here, again, MacIntyre appears to agree with our position. For the most part, practices exist in a society because they contribute to it. Consequently, moral virtues will be consistent with the teleology of the society.

However, MacIntyre attempts to distinguish his theory from utilitarian teleology. He argues that the utilitarian regards moral behavior as aimed at external goods, those to be attained as the result of virtuous activity, such as the candy that the child acquires in learning chess, rather than internal goods, such as courage, for its own sake, in a society that recognizes practices requiring courage (p. 185).

We find unconvincing MacIntyre's argument distinguishing himself from utilitarianism. He claims that virtue in a society can be at odds with happiness, but his reasons are not compelling. As examples, he points out that one does not always benefit by virtuous action; courage, honesty, and justice can lead to misery. However, the examples do not refute utilitarianism but egoism. The utilitarian does not expect the agent of moral action to benefit. Utilitarianism is aimed at the happiness of society rather than the individual.

But even when the happiness of the society does not result from virtuous action, the utilitarian has an explanation. As Rawls, Hare, and Brandt argued, utilitarianism, in a sophisticated form, recognizes that occasionally actions in keeping with the generally reliable moral practices may have exceptions. In such cases, however, those three philosophers argue that one ought to stay the course because, all things considered, keeping to the general practice usually is ultimately beneficial despite the occasional exception. MacIntyre appears to have overlooked Rawls's utilitarian use of the distinction between justification of a practice and justification within the practice

The same considerations apply to MacIntyre's objection that utilitarianism promotes actions aimed at external goods rather than internal. Utilitarianism is committed to nothing of the sort. As Rawls, Hare, and Brandt have argued, a society may be ultimately better off if its members seek virtue for its own sake. Aristotelian teleology, which MacIntyre claims largely to accept, values virtue as an end in itself, although it is ultimately justified by its benefit to the society

MacIntyre is also deontological. If, as we have maintained, teleology and deontology are different descriptions of the same morality, and if, as we now argue, MacIntyre is teleological in the manner of a well-developed utilitarianism, his theory must also be implicitly deontological. No better evidence for that deontology can be found than in MacIntyre's observation that there appears to be, despite the diversity of different societies, a nearly universal virtue: "integrity or consistency" (p. 189).

We regard MacIntyre's attempt to deny his implicit utilitarianism as flawed, yet flawed in an instructive way. Although his own position does the reverse, he argues that utilitarian action is aimed at an external good, while incidentally producing actions usually considered as internal goods. But we argue that the difference is precisely that of describing the same underlying moral reality in two different ways. Let us return to our analogy of colors and light waves to exemplify our point. Suppose, for example, that a computer screen displays colors that result from mixing colors that are painted on keys on the keyboard. The keyboard may not have a specific shade of maroon, but it has a brown and a red that can be combined to produce maroon. The keys also have, printed on them, the wavelength of its color. The screen displays not only the color that is produced but also its wavelength.

We now ask the artist, who has a phobia of numbers, and a color-blind scientist to produce the same color on their identical computers. The artist uses his color sense and manipulates the keys accordingly. The scientist cannot see colors, so he relies entirely upon the numerical equivalents. But his movements and their results are identical to those of the artist. Were they doing the same thing or different things? Each would describe his actions differently from the other because they observed the same phenomenon of color under different description. Yet, their actions can be entirely consistent with each other, with each participant accomplishing the same result.

MacIntyre describes the virtuous person as pursuing virtue, for its own sake, while coincidentally producing, for the most part, social happiness. He describes the utilitarian—at least in a form less sophisticated than that described by Rawls, Hare, and Brandt—as seeking social happiness while behaving, for the most part, virtuously. MacIntyre's virtuous person and his utilitarian are like the artist and the scientist.

The deontologist is the third member of our unity, so we must make room for him in our computer example. We introduce a third person who is blind. However, the computer can translate light waves into sound waves, and he is asked to produce the sound corresponding to the color that was requested of the artist and scientist. The rest of the example need not be elaborated.

It may be objected that the teleologist, deontologist, and character-based theorist will not always agree, as will our computer users. However, the computer users could disagree also. The artist's color perception is not perfect, nor is the blind person's sense of hearing. Although numbers are very precise, some numerical values, such as irrational numbers, can never be expressed exactly. Consequently, even our scientist experiences uncertainty. They disagree because they are imperfect observers. So also are human beings, whether they consider morals from the perspective of teleology, deontology, or character theory. The person least likely to err on the computer screen would be someone who observed it from all three perspectives. So, also, would the best moral observer examine all three moral perspectives both to allow them to correct each other and to permit himself to compile all analyses into a consistent whole.

Intuitionism as Part of the Unity

We are left with intuitionism. Intuitionism is difficult to analyze because, by its own self-description, it leaves little to analyze. For the intuitionist, moral judgments are made purely from a moral sense, without need of explanation. Intuitionists claim to discern moral good or evil through a "moral sense," as people discern color by the sense of sight, an analogy proposed by G. E. Moore (1966) in his famous essay "The Subject Matter of Ethics" (p. 74)

Intuitionism has considerable appeal. In most cases, people do not need to analyze actions such as stealing, cheating, murder, or, on the positive side, generosity, to determine their moral standing. People would be content, in most cases, merely to say, "I know that it is right (or wrong), and I need not prove or intellectually expound on the matter." Furthermore, the moral intuitions play an important role in the analysis of moral theories. When one evaluates a moral theory, one examines the behavior that it approves and disapproves to determine if he or she finds the theory attractive. However tightly reasoned the theory may be, one is tempted to reject it if it recommends behavior that one finds unacceptable. The traditional problems of utilitarianism and Kantianism arise because there are cases in which each theory seems, *prima facie*, to offend our moral sensibilities. The utilitarian must defend against claims that he is too lax with moral rules, and the Kantian must defend against the charge of rigidity. People rely so heavily upon the "moral sensitivity" that it cannot be ignored by any serious moral theorist.

We must ask the intuitionist to explain why the intuitions are valid. If no explanation is forthcoming, we must wonder if the alleged intuitions are merely subjective feelings with no objective import. In responding to such requests, the intuitionist invariably enters the teleology–deontology–character-based complex.

Moore (1951) answers in a manner strongly suggestive of utilitarian teleology. He denies the validity of the utilitarian definition, or moreover, any definition, of the word "good," and concludes that good is a property distinct from happiness or its production. However, on consulting his own intuitions, he finds that they approve of actions that promote human happiness (pp. 146–147). Thus Moore disputes the utilitarian definition of "good" but applies that adjective to the same actions that the utilitarian considers good. Here the blend of teleology and deontology in intuitionism is evident. Intuitionism is essentially deontological because it regards acts as good or bad merely on the basis of their possession of a moral property and not on the basis of their consequences. Yet, as John Hill (1976) remarks, Moore's intuitions lead him to approve essentially utilitarian behavior. Moore (1951) argues that, as a matter of observable fact, things that have the property of being good also happen to promote teleological happiness, and that the best actions are those with the best consequences (pp. 146–147).

A Unified Approach to the Consideration of Ethical Issues

Why do theorists insist on subsuming all of ethics, in its many facets, under one limited theory? The Kantian wishes to examine all of ethics and all aspects of it from an exclusively Kantian viewpoint, while regarding all other viewpoints as alien and mistaken. The utilitarian, character-based theorist, and intuitionist likewise claim exclusivity. It is as if the biologist, psychologist, physician, physicist, chemist, and poet were each to claim complete and exclusive understanding of a human being.

But, aside from mere parochialism, there may be a more substantive tendency at work: the desire to subsume an entire subject matter under a single explanation. It is possible that attempts to unify ethics entirely under one system of explanation may, ironically, have prevented people from noticing the more encompassing unity that results when more limited theories are united with each other. Each of the supposedly competing theories contains a unified explanation, and it is natural enough to wish to include an entire subject matter under one uniting principle. However, to suppose that any single such principle excludes all others is to ignore the possibility of a grander unity.

That unity may be found in the nature of the human being, who displays all of the characteristics discussed by the ethical theorists we have considered. Human beings have a unique respect for principle as such, whether found in mathematics, physics, or ethics. Principles explain things in a manner that the rational part of a human being understands, and principles express the consistency of behavior that people expect from each other. Kant ingeniously develops that human aspect. But there is also an emotional side of humanity that Kant ignores. The utilitarian teleologist acknowledges the side of us that desires happiness for ourselves and, with the exception of some people all of the time and all people some of the time, in others. We live in societies and naturally value behavior with a positive social consequence. As Hume (1951, p. 417) argues, there is a benevolent passion in people that approves altruistic behavior but reviles malevolent action. There is also a third side of human beings that respects great achievement whether in art, athletics, or science. That side of us considers a person's life as a creative work judged by his or her character traits. And there is also a side that occasionally shouts, "I know but I cannot and need not explain." Human beings could not exist without reliance on such unexplained intuitions. If we waited for explanation and certainty in all situations, we would scarcely ever act or hold a belief. Deontology, teleology, character-based theories, and intuitionism all discuss aspects of a human being, but each discusses only a single aspect. All are unified in human nature.

Humanity could not have evolved so successfully if all of those aspects were independent. The physical parts of a human being have evolved to work together in mutual dependence. Human beings would be strange evolution-defying natural enigmas if their inherent mental functions were naturally in conflict rather than in unity. Human reasoning, love of happiness, benevolence, respect for moral character, and intuitive reactions are almost certainly parts of a unified, evolved human nature. If so, deontology, teleology, character theory, and intuitionism must be in a unified harmony.

We are left with some unfinished business. Now that we have argued that there is a fundamental unity in human ethics, we must discuss how to use that unity to address ethical problems. We do not attempt to provide a formula to solve them all in computer-like fashion. As we saw, interpretations of Kant falter because they seek to make his investigation of the foundations of ethical thinking into such a formula. Instead, we attempt to show how the uniting of the different perspectives can be used to guide ethical thinking, as a system of mutual correctives that direct human judgment toward moral resolution.

Let us take, as an example, a case of the sort that proved troublesome to Kant. An angry man wielding a weapon asks if his intended victim, who is hiding from the assailant, is present. The person of whom the request is made knows that the intended victim is present and knows what is likely to occur. Is he duty-bound to tell the truth? Kant's rigid deontology would appear to answer "Yes," because to answer otherwise would be a lie. Utilitarians would object that happiness would be best served by the benevolent lie. Our moral intuitions would clearly hold with the utilitarian in this case. It is because most people share those intuitions that the case is so difficult for Kant. Character-based theory could also be interpreted to support the lie. A character-based theorist might argue that no one of good character would assist one person in the murder of another, despite the need to lie. Disregard for human life is a worse character trait than the propensity to lie to save a life. Such lying would not amount to dishonesty of character. But if we are correct in supposing that ethics forms a unity among all of these theories, the Kantian must somehow be understood to agree.

The situation is one of particular significance to our theory of unification. It demonstrates how agreement among some of the ethical perspectives can guide interpretation of another. Once convincing evidence from those sources in agreement can be presented, they provide a context for the interpretation of the apparent maverick. With regard to the example in question, we can apply the latitude that Sullivan sees in Kant to good advantage. We can now ask which course of action, lying or telling the truth to a person intent on murder, best exhibits the categorical imperative. Would the lie or the truth best treat human beings as ends in themselves? One could answer either way in a manner consistent with Kant's overall theory. To lie would express the value of human life, in itself; but, in depriving the potential murderer of his freedom to make a choice, the lie would not treat him as an end in himself. Kantianism, attempting to stand entirely on its own, cannot determine the issue. But in our analysis, Kantianism need not stand entirely on its own. With guidance from the other theories in the unity, the appropriate interpretation of Kantianism becomes evident. The lie that defends an innocent life against a person controlled by animalistic emotions expresses the intrinsic value of human life more fully.

Another example can be used to show how the teleological position can be reinterpreted in light of *prima facie* disagreement with the other ethical theories. Let us suppose that, in order to solve a terrible drug abuse problem, a government decides that happiness for society would result from stern punishment for drug use. The penalty for possession of any drug, including marijuana, is death. The policy is instituted and is, on the surface, successful. Five hundred petty drug users and a few innocent but suspected abusers are executed over five years. Drug abuse is fully eradicated, and drug dealers lose their business. The teleologist would seem forced either to argue that the policy is good or resort to the confused rule utilitarianism. The Kantian would decry the policy as unjustly using human beings, some of whom are entirely innocent, as means. The Kantian would also object to a punishment so inconsistent with the crime. Human intuitions would also seem revolted at such heavy-handed rule. The character theorist would ask, "What kind of people would do this, and what kind of character models are they providing for the society?" How could the utilitarian truly hold to such brutality?

The utilitarian need not institute such brutal tactics. There is latitude in utilitarianism as there is in Kantianism. The utilitarian could examine the entire context of the case and recognize the resentment against government that the policy would engender. The resentment would arise precisely because it offended the very aspects of human beings that are developed philosophically by Kant, character-based theorists, and intuitionists. A society so revolted by its own government's policies, no matter how successful they seem to be, risks utter disintegration. Furthermore, the success of such brutal policies develops a tendency to use such brutality to solve other problems and thus degenerate into a tyranny. A utilitarian could consider all of these and other possible negative consequences and conclude that the policy should not be instituted.

Thus, the utilitarian can give two possible answers to the question of whether the policy should be instituted. The utilitarian is in much the same position as the Kantian of the previous example. Utilitarianism, on its own, cannot resolve the issue. But the clear message of the Kantian, with the support of the intuitionist and of the character-based theorist, provides the direction in which the utilitarian may look for an answer.

We do not mean to suggest that apparent disagreements among the ethical theories should be decided by a majority rule among them. Sometimes one is so much more convincing on its own merits that it governs the interpretation of the others. For example, when the Miranda decision was first issued by the Supreme Court, it offended many people's senses, or intuitions, of justice. The character of the defendant, Miranda, was also offensive to many. The utilitarian might argue that the effect of the decision was to make law enforcement more difficult and thus damage the society. However, the Kantian insistence that people are not to be manipulated but treated as ends in themselves bears the clearest message. Given that message, the intuitions, in a more reflective posture, would recognize the injustice of depriving someone of knowledge of his legal rights and then abusing his ignorance of them. The utilitarian would notice that a society that abused the rights even of loathsome criminals would severely injure itself. The character-based theorist would turn her attention to improving the characters of law enforcement agents, who are far more representative of the society as a whole, as well as to the character of the marginal criminal. The clear deontological message can thus be translated to the other aspects of ethical thought.

There is no formula, be it majority rule among the theories or some mathematical schema, for applying the system of ethics as a unity. There is no substitute for the use of good judgment in the application of any system to particular cases. Ethics is more art than science. Yet, ethics is far from unique in this respect. Courts of law, including the Supreme Court of the United States, must make judgments based on the law but not precisely inferred from the law. There is often disagreement among judges concerning how law applies, but agreement concerning support for the laws themselves. The laws cannot establish formulaic rules regarding their own interpretation and application. But the laws constitute the context for a legal decision, determining what is relevant to the decision and upon what factors the decision is to be rendered. While the laws may permit a degree of uncertainty, without them, decisions would be arbitrary and without foundation. Similarly, the unity of ethical theories cannot make all ethical decisions, but it can guide them.

There is also another benefit to the application of the ethical theories in their unity. Once they are understood in conformity with each other and applied to a case in mutual consistency, the ethical act can be reasonably explained in a comprehensive manner. The explanation, if compelling, elicits agreement from its audience, be they supervisors, subordinates, the public that is served, or their representatives; defends the moral agent from charges of arbitrariness or worse; and serves as a model for other decisions and moral agents. Within a public organization, all three functions are of self-explanatory significance.

Conclusion

Moral decisions were made long before philosophers began to analyze them, and most decisions, such as Lincoln's signing of the Emancipation Proclamation, are still made without consulting philosophers or their theories. One must bear in mind that morality is the preexisting and independently existing subject of philosophic analysis and not the creation of the philosopher. No single ethical theory, be it deontological, teleological, character-based, or intuitionist, determines ethics, but, rather, ethical behavior is the subject matter that those theories are called upon to enlighten. The nature of the beast determines how we should analyze it, rather than the reverse.

Each of the theories that we have discussed enlightens an aspect of ethics, but none encompasses ethics in its entirety. Perhaps there are even aspects that all four taken together cannot include; one must not preclude new sources of ethical knowledge in the future. Until such new sources are discovered, the moral mind recognizes the value of all four in their unity.

Although all perspectives are of roughly equal value in the reckonings of the moral mind, there is a special intellectual role that is fulfilled by Kantian deontology. Human beings are rational and, as such, demand answers to their questions. Fishkin (1984) remarks that some Yale students, when confronted with ethical values, skeptically demand an explanation of how any ultimate value can be justified (p. 37). If one value is justified by means of another, the original skepticism is merely transferred to the justifying value. One always demands a final explanation. Kant uniquely supplies rational finality. He reduces morality to logical consistency, and one cannot rationally ask "Why should I be consistent?" or more basically "Why should I be moral?" The self-defeating nature of such a question is immediately recognized by the rational moral mind.

In the fifth and final chapter, we attempt to apply our integrated objective ethics to public administration. We focus, first, on the essential elements of the administrative role—agency and autonomy—and offer a four-step framework to promote ethical analysis and action. Second, we examine a specific case of administrative behavior to illustrate the applicability of our integrated perspective; and third, we address the false dichotomies between the bureaucratic ethos and the democratic ethos and bureaucracy and democracy, respectively. Our argument is that moral agency, grounded in the integrated objective ethics, provides a philosophical and practical basis for the reconciliation of these dichotomies and the creation of a new normative identity and legitimacy for public administration.

5

Ethical Unity in Public Administration

Is ethics job-related? Can ethical competence be included in a job description along with computer skills, problem-solving ability, and willingness to be a team player? The answer to these questions is clearly yes. But to many public administration academics and practitioners, the question is either never asked or, if considered at all, is answered legalistically or simply no. To the extent that there is any consciousness of the issues embedded in these questions, the answer might be that values are addressed in the political process, thus absolving administrators of any moral responsibility in their professional pursuits. Yet, the political process tends to address values only in an abbreviated or truncated sense, often in response to interest-group–driven goals and priorities. Therefore, if broader, more comprehensive constitutional and philosophical values are to be addressed consistently by government, it must occur largely in the bureaucracy.

We must ask, however, what warrants bureaucratic involvement in values as opposed to only technocratic issues? The philosophical and constitutional answer, in our view, is bureaucrats' individual status and responsibility as moral actors as well as their commitment to regime values. On the practical level, electorally addressed values cannot resolve management-related issues, and on the policy level, once legislation is enacted, a vast array of ethical issues pervade the planning, implementation, and evaluation processes. Thus, the bureaucrats directly and daily enmeshed in these processes bear a responsibility to take these ethical issues into account. At this juncture, however, we might ask whether all bureaucrats are equally obligated in this regard. In our judgment, the answer is yes and no: yes in the context of moral principles that we all share; no in the context of the degree of moral awareness and experience of particular individuals. Although all human beings are moral actors, consideration of the nuances, subtleties, and implications of ethical issues in public administration must be modeled and led by those bureaucrats who are morally literate, technically adept, and politically astute. It would be unreasonable to expect a young, inexperienced bureaucrat to take the lead in this connection.

Our argument in this chapter is that the integrated ethical perspective delineated in chapter 4 can be a vehicle to help the public administrator become, at once, a more effective democrat and technocrat. If it is reasonable to expect public administrators to act ethically while simultaneously acting technocratically, then, by definition, public administrators are granted discretion. To be moral is to exercise discretion and judgment. But what is meant by "act ethically" and what are the sources of ethical action? By "act ethically" we mean that public administrators who adopt our integrated stance will internalize a perspective that comprehends the ethical and technical aspects of their duties and obligations, and that enables them to express, reflect, and advocate normative concerns in both management and policy. They will operate from a coherent moral point of view. The sources of ethical action include one's upbringing, background, and observations of important figures in one's life, as well as education and training, including formal academic programs and organizational seminars and workshops.

The unified moral perspective is grounded in the actual nature of administrative circumstances. Where managers are, the facts they face, the constraints they confront, all condition the values of our moral perspective. The adoption and application of the integrated objective ethics model is intended to assist public administrators in their thinking, deciding, and acting. It is intended to strengthen the public service by institutionalizing and internalizing an ethical point of view. It is not intended merely to address moral dilemmas or quandaries, conflicts of roles and obligations. It is also intended to ensure routine ethical analysis, dialogue, decision making, and justification. The dialogue itself, of course, is only a process. While intersubjective discourse and community are important, the moral basis of such discourse and community must be continually explicated.

The unified moral perspective is embedded in the nature of managerial reality. It assumes that public administrators share with other human beings an intuitive moral sense, which provides a backdrop to their decisions and actions. This intuitive sense, while often inchoate, is ever-present and requires nurturance and clarification to be activated. The public service will be ethically enlivened only if moral passivists become moral activists, if the values at stake in any given situation are delineated as clearly as possible, considered as fairly as possible, and fulfilled as much as possible. In no way, however, are we suggesting moral certainty. Instead, we are trying to provide a framework, which practitioners, in particular, may find helpful in unraveling the moral mysteries of their environment and detecting those ethical clues that may lead to policy and management clarity grounded in a comprehensive grasp of the challenges they confront.

We saw in chapter 3 that several public administration scholars such as Stewart (1984), Denhardt (1988), Guy (1991), Lewis (1991), Chandler (1994), Pops (1994), and Frederickson (1997), recognize a deontological–teleological connection. We also saw that Dobel (1998) suggests that laws, norms, and duties are enlivened by virtue, and that Cooper (1987) believes that a complete normative ethics for public administration includes ethical principles, virtues supportive of those principles, and analytical techniques to interpret those principles. We also saw that Pugh (1991) sees the bureaucratic ethos and democratic ethos, which constitute the principal framework of public management ethics, as teleological and deontological, respectively. Therefore, some groundwork already had been laid for our unified moral perspective. These and other administrative ethicists have grappled with the fundamental moral issues in public administration and have enriched our understanding in the process. What has not yet been achieved, however, is the reconciliation of these seemingly disparate philosophical positions and its application to administrative practice. In our view, such a reconciliation is crucial and can be effected at both the philosophical and practical levels primarily because we all naturally seek meaning and integrity in both our personal and professional lives. Reconciliation, we believe, is the product of a universal and timeless moral impulse. As David Schmidtz (1995) has said, "[m]oral imperatives have a characteristic importance and urgency in virtue of being grounded in principles that are very general, nonarbitrary, and at the heart of what makes it possible for human beings to flourish in communities" (p. 25).

In its unification of deontology, teleology, virtue ethics, and intuitionism, chapter 4 showed the underlying inseparability of these positions. It also showed that the artificial and arbitrary divisions among them simply fragment our thinking, decision making, and action. This fragmentation, in turn, serves no useful purpose beyond the analytical. Therefore, although deontology, teleology, virtue, and intuitionism may be deconstructed for the sake of deliberation and dialogue, their essential unity must be distilled and captured for coherent decision making, policy, and practice.

Here, in chapter 5, we first consider the relationship between our unified moral perspective and administrative agency and autonomy—the fundamental ingredients in the administrative role. In this connection, we review the work of Henry Kass, Gary Wamsley, Philip Jos, and Terry Cooper. Our aim is to demonstrate the application of our integrated moral perspective to the issues raised in the literature. We are interested in showing how our perspective can help resolve those issues by its invocation of a unified philosophical foundation that, in turn, can help administrators to articulate an understanding of moral connections and to sustain moral convictions as they attempt to meet their policy and management responsibilities. We then present a specific case to illustrate the applicability of our moral perspective to administrative circumstances, and we conclude with a proposed reconciliation of both the bureaucratic ethos–democratic ethos dichotomy and the bureaucracy–democracy dilemma.

Agency and Autonomy

Kass (1989) provides a point of departure for a consideration of agency theory in the public sector. He defines agency as a normative theory of how one person should act for another and contends that it frames much of our thinking about administrative ethics. Indeed, agency is crucial to a coherent theory of ethics in public administration. In the public sector, the principal is usually the citizenry; agents are administrators who act through agencies; and third parties are those subject to administrative action. But what seems to interest Kass in particular is the possibility or even the probability of abuse in public sector principal–agent relations. "The potential for injustice being committed in an agency relationship increases in a number of ways when the power of the state is involved" (p. 952).

Agents can take advantage of principals' ignorance of their work and inability to monitor their activities; principals can deny agents their personal and ethical autonomy by requiring and coercing them to do things they believe are unjust; third parties can be injured and unjustly treated by agents acting either in collusion with principals or beyond their authority. Thus, the norms of agency attempt to reduce the vulnerability of all parties to unjust treatment by one another.

According to Kass, agency norms reduce vulnerability in two ways: They establish special obligations between agent and principal designed to prevent exploitation and abuse, and they subordinate these obligations to a universal justice norm. Ethical public administrators are required by these general obligations not to act unjustly toward others. This requirement, in turn, limits any special obligations owed by the principal and agent to one another. Moreover, Kass argues that underlying the concept of agency are a number of special norms governing the principal–agent relationship itself. For example, the special ethical obligation of the agent to honor his or her promise to achieve the principal's welfare first is the fiduciary norm. An agent's loyalty to the principal's trust, which includes full disclosure, diligence, and judgment, is grounded in the fiduciary norm. A second special norm inherent in the principal–agent relationship concerns agent integrity, which circumscribes the principal's requests or demands of the agent. Agency theory, therefore, recognizes the agent's moral autonomy and integrity. Indeed, Kass believes that agency provides administrators a basis both to evaluate claims and counterclaims on their loyalty and to establish an ethical identity that emphasizes the personal responsibility of each agent. Finally, Kass notes three problems in using agency theory: (1) the limited ethical roles of the agent in the traditional Wilsonian model of public administration; (2) the interposition of organizational culture and values between the agent and the public as principal; and (3) the lack of a viable concept of the public interest in American politics. He concludes that agency must rise above its Wilsonian roots, that public organizations must become public agencies that take seriously the fiduciary, agent integrity, and justice norms, and, most importantly, the perennial public interest problem must be addressed. Otherwise, Kass contends, "there is no legitimate principal in a democratic state for which agents can act, and no form of legitimate business they can pursue in the name of the public" (p. 965).

Kass (1990) notes that agent norms have been characterized as means to instrumentalize a person or organizational agent and make her an amoral tool at the principal's disposal. According to this view, agency short-circuits an agent's individual or organizational responsibility as an ethical actor, allowing the actor to justify even heinous acts in the principal's name. Kass argues, however, that an ethical system of agency is not susceptible to this criticism, since fiduciary norms are limited by considerations of justice, beneficence, and respect for the agent's own personal or organizational integrity. "All the specific norms of agency," Kass maintains, "are basically applications of universal justice and beneficence norms to agency settings. All specific norms, including fiduciary norms, are judged by how well they effectuate these universal obligations in agency" (p. 119). Furthermore, unlike those who believe that complex organizations as agents or principals nullify the ethical aspect of the representative, Kass suggests that complex organizations can take the moral point of view. A moral point of view requires rationality, the ability to frame one's projects and understand their implications for others, and respect for others as ends in themselves.

With regard to the application of agency theory to the public sector, Kass refers to Joseph Tussman's *Obligation and the Body Politic* (1960) in which Tussman suggests that agency is central to the modern theory of the state. A democratic state, according to Tussman, is an association formed to pursue the common interests of the participants. In the association, individuals and groups play two roles: (1) as members, in which they receive benefits of membership, and (2) as agents, in which they are required to act on behalf of the shared interests of members of the state. Without agency, therefore, the state is impotent, and the *res publica* goes undone. Moreover, in a democratic state, the principal is the people, the republic, or the taxpayers. Agents are those who act on behalf of the state through any kind of decision-making institution—they may be legislators, chief elected executives, or administrators.

Kass also writes of the two problems associated with agency theory, one common to all agency-based concepts, the other unique to the notion of agency in a pluralist democracy. The common problem is vulnerability, which increases in the public sector because of agency power. Indeed, the legitimation crisis is rooted in the citizen's fear of public agents abusing others while justifying themselves in terms of service to the public. In Kass's judgment, fiduciary and agent integrity norms play the major role in alleviating the problem of mutual vulnerability in the republic.

The second problem with agency theory lies in the nature of pluralist democracy. Some believe that it is unrealistic to use the agency ethic as a standard of public service because they feel it is impossible to identify a public principal with a coherent identity or interest. Kass counters that the pluralists are right if the public principal is sought in group process and kaleidoscopic politics. If, however, attention moves to the basic political association and process that give coherence to the pluralist political system itself, then the principal and interest may be found. What must be sought, therefore, is the unity that characterizes the republic. Focusing on the republic, on the underlying association and common civic understanding in pluralism, provides the identity of the principal and the principal's interest necessary to support an operational agency ethic. Finally, Kass suggests that "[a]gency . . . links the abstractions of ethics, constitution, self, and organization to the concrete daily practice of those public agents who serve us" (p. 125).

Wamsley (1990) suggests that a normative guide for the cultivation of public virtues should conceptualize the public administrator as an agent acting on behalf of others in a vigorous and thoughtful manner and should build an autonomous agential role based on unique claims for a special role in governance. These claims should include: (1) expertise in operationalizing policy in the form of specific programs; (2) expertise in creating and sustaining processes and dialogue that results in the broadest definition of the public interest; (3) skills in community-building politics and the fostering of active citizenship; and (4) guardianship along with other constitutional officers of the Constitution and constitutional processes. An agent, in Wamsley's view, is an active or efficient cause, exerts power, is responsible for his acts, is a means or instrument by which a guiding intelligence achieves a result, and acts for or in the place of another by authority from him. The agential perspective requires public administrators to see themselves as citizen agents standing in place of other citizen principals, exerting power for them and in their stead to achieve an end, a collective purpose, always consciously responsible to them and acting by their authority.

For public administrators to be seen as legitimate agents, the agency must be committed to the broadest possible definition of the public interest derivable from its statutory mandate, fiduciary responsibility, and consistency with the Constitution. The agency must either satisfy or balance powerful interests, and it must represent the unspoken interests of unwitting stakeholders. The agency must pursue a common good that is distinguishable from what a society thinks it wants; that is, assuming that society's wishes are manifest in constitutionally correct laws, agential leadership must follow the law while continuing to educate citizens toward the common good until the shape of the issues becomes clear. In the end, the public administrator's role is that of an autonomous subordinate, an agent responsive and responsible to the people as well as to officials and institutions, oriented toward the common good, the agency's mission, and active citizenship.

Jos (1988) argues that modern organizations erode the individual's capacity for independent thinking and decision making. He maintains that "something even more fundamental than freedom is at stake" (p. 323), namely, the ability of employees to decide what they should do. In their deference to others, in fact, they "may become party to immoral or illegal activities and policies" (p. 323). The central issue in this context is "the worker's autonomy, his status as a chooser" (p. 323).

In Jos's view, there are both internal and external obstacles to autonomous judgment. They range from physiological impairments to psychological weaknesses to emotions and passions, on the internal side, to severe forms of manipulation such as brainwashing, to more typical forms of manipulation such as socialization into organizational roles, on the external side. Jos believes that "the ambiguity of typical decision contexts can be an important obstacle to autonomous judgment as well" (p. 325).

Jos (1988) suggests that autonomy "requires not so much cognition and obedience, i.e., respect for moral law, as a more complete strength of character" (p. 325). Citing Richard Dagger, for whom autonomy is "the ability to control our lives through reasoned choice," Jos also draws on Aristotle and his "sensitivity to the complexities of moral choice" (p. 325). True moral knowledge, in Aristotle's judgment, means that doing what is right "must spring from a firm and unchangeable character" (p. 326). Moral autonomy requires not only a belief in moral principles but also ownership of those principles in a more fundamental way. Beliefs and standards must become part of one's character, which, in turn, involves "moral sensitivity, understanding, and courage" (p. 326). Knowing the difference between right and wrong or believing in common moral precepts is necessary but not sufficient for moral autonomy. What is also required is the willingness and ability to define a situation as calling for a moral choice. While Jos (1988) contends that "autonomy requires self-discipline and self-control" (p. 323), he expresses misgivings about Kant's notion of the autonomy of the will. Our moral experience should not be considered "simply another variety of duty versus inclination" (p. 323). In Jos's judgment, in fact, it is dangerous to do so. Moreover, Jos interprets Kant, with his putative commitment to unconditional moral laws, as leaving no room for independent decision making. Jos claims that "Kant's only recourse is to define autonomy as respect for and obedience to the moral law because it *is* the moral law" (p. 324). Autonomy is equivalent to conformity to unconditional laws. Finally, however, in a footnote citing Roger Sullivan, Jos acknowledges that Kant neither approved of individuals acting as automatons, nor took pleasure in pedants who could not think for themselves. Jos's position is that Kant underspecified typical decision contexts and had a narrow view of human nature, which was of little help in understanding motivation, discipline, and moral character. According to Jos (1988), "[t]he Kantian moral agent learns deference, obedience, and respect, capacities which are unlikely to help him or her think and act autonomously in the face of ambiguity or manipulation by others" (p. 324).

In a later essay on administrative responsibility, moral consensus, and moral autonomy, Jos (1990) argues that public administration's attempts to develop an account of the morally responsible administrator have been disappointing. The root of the problem lies in the precarious status of public administration in a liberal society. In Jos's view, public administration's persistent defense of administrative discretion as its commitment to the public interest has distorted efforts to formulate a viable theory of administrative responsibility. Such a theory, he believes, is a function of the moral character of public administrators. Jos also refers to our capacity for rationalization and self-deception in defining work situations as requiring a moral choice. Thus, the pursuit of self-interest is not the only or even the most important barrier to a responsible public service, and the administrator is not always confronted by obvious corruption or conduct that is reprehensible under any circumstances. Moral ambiguity is the norm along with ambiguity in authority. Finally, in perhaps an inadvertent Kantian vein, Jos says that "[e]xercising autonomy is not freedom to interpret the moral good as one sees fit; it is exercising the sensitivity, understanding, and courage necessary to fully and independently consider obligations to clients, superiors, elected officials, the Constitution, and fundamental principles in the course of one's duties" (p. 244).

Cooper (1990), too, is concerned with autonomy and the role of organizations in its suppression. For Cooper, there are three ingredients essential to maintaining limits on our administrative responsibility and loyalty to an organization: (1) Work organizations must be delimited and an identity cultivated that transcends their boundaries; (2) legal and institutional mechanisms must be established for constraining organizational power and protecting individual rights to exercise ethical autonomy; and (3) self-awareness of our rights, duties, values, and obligations is required. Cooper is especially concerned about the so-called agentic shift—the transition from autonomous to organizational functioning—the effect of which is that individuals no longer regard themselves as responsible for their own actions. Instead, they submit to authority and take pride in compliance. A moral act is reduced to obedience to authority.

To illustrate the impact of organizations on individual ethical autonomy, Cooper briefly discusses William H. Whyte's 1956 work, *The Organization Man,* and William Scott and David K. Hart's 1979 work,
Organizational America. While he finds both provocative, although in-
conclusive, Cooper cites as more sophisticated and theoretically complex
Alberto Guerreiro Ramos's (1981) *The New Science of Organizations: A
Reconceptualization of the Wealth of Nations,* which is a critique of instrumental rationality. Cooper says that he cites these three works to suggest
the importance of bounding organizational loyalties and commitments if
we are to maintain any degree of ethical autonomy. Organizations, in his
view, are too frequently allowed to occupy a predominant position in
people's lives, resulting in their self-esteem and dignity being based in the
workplace. Therefore, Cooper's work links autonomy and agency, although his interest is limited to finding ways to avoid the agentic shift and
thus the erosion of autonomy.

A common feature in the work of Kass, Wamsley, Jos, and Cooper
is the absence of an explicit moral basis for agent autonomy. While
Kass, for example, argues that agency is crucial to a coherent theory of
ethics in public administration, he provides no clear intellectual or moral
foundation for such a theory. Agency, he tells us, is a normative theory
of how one person should act for another and forms much of our
thinking about administrative ethics. But beyond brief Kantian-like
references to a universal justice norm that applies to ethical public
administrators and to the capacity of complex organizations to adopt a
moral point of view, which requires rationality, Kass offers little as to
the nature of agency theory or its relationship to agent autonomy.
Although he writes of the fiduciary norm, which obligates the agent to
achieve the principal's welfare, and a second norm concerning agent
integrity, his treatment of these issues is tautological, at best. For example, after asserting that this second norm in the principal–agent relationship circumscribes the principal's requests or demands of the agent,
he concludes that agency, therefore, recognizes the agent's moral autonomy and integrity. While the practical effect of this norm may be as

described on one level, its underlying rationale and link to agent autonomy is not apparent from Kass's circular reasoning.

Wamsley's justification of agent autonomy is based on the public administrator's expertise and position—essentially the truncated professional autonomy of the attorney, physician, or engineer. It is the autonomy of the elite whose specialized knowledge and experience provide a privileged vantage point for shaping and administering policies and programs, guiding dialogue and citizenship development, and acting as surrogates for less-advantaged citizens in a quest for the public interest. A special role in governance and a special understanding of the common good constitute the agential perspective. But, again, no underlying moral rationale is offered to justify expertise or position as the basis for agent autonomy.

Jos mentions critiques of the modern organization's adverse impact on individual autonomy but cites no specific sources or evidence, nor does he provide any moral basis or explanation of autonomy. Although he refers to Kant, his analysis is both conventional and confused—conventional in its attribution to Kant of a commitment to mindless duty, confused in its acknowledgment that Kant approved of neither automatons nor pedants. Then, in an attempt to extricate himself from this inconsistency, Jos posits that Kant's problem is his underspecification of decision contexts and his narrow view of human nature. But as we have shown, Kant's conception of human nature was quite complex and frequently enriched by specific examples of human behavior. Jos's own Kantian suggestion of what the exercise of autonomy entails actually demonstrates the fullness of Kant's view.

Cooper, like Jos, emphasizes the putative organizational impediments to autonomy rather than its moral basis. His concern about the agentic shift assumes but does not explain initial individual autonomy, which he claims is inevitably transformed by organizational norms into conscienceless subordination. Indeed, Cooper's description of the human result of the agentic shift is reminiscent of the caricature of Kant's obedient servant. Further, Cooper's argument would have been strengthened by specific evidence of the agentic shift in contemporary public organizations. Unfortunately, no such evidence is supplied. Instead, he offers only the dated anxieties of William Whyte, William Scott, and David Hart, and the familiar Milgram experiments. Moreover, with respect to Cooper's concern about practitioners whose psychic investment in their organizations is excessive and his recommendation that we bracket our organizational loyalties, there seems to be some confusion. If, in fact, some individuals try to find the meaning of life in their workplaces, it may be a function of their own personalities rather than a reflection of organizational repression. Finally, in the context of the contemporary academic disregard for the politics–administration dichotomy, one must wonder why Cooper evinces so much concern about the agentic shift. If at least some public administrators participate in major policy and management decisions, then in what sense may we claim that they have made the agentic shift? For public administrators at certain levels, the dissolution of the politics–administration dichotomy seems to imply the dissolution of the potential for an agentic shift.

We now come to the relationship between our unified moral perspective and the literature on administrative agency and autonomy. While we acknowledge the scholarly contributions to our understanding of these essential elements in public administration theory and practice, we believe that what is required at this point is a fuller examination of the moral nature, dimensions, and implications of agency and autonomy in the administrative environment. The unified objective ethics is inseparable from the public administrator's three roles as agent, expert, and steward; and activating or applying these connections in the management and policy arenas can provide the administrator with a coherent moral perspective. This perspective, in turn, can enable more effective dialogue, deliberation, and justification of decisions and actions. Principled purpose, conduct, and consequence are indivisible. The hats of the agent, the expert, and the steward are worn simultaneously by the administrator as an autonomous, authentic, and accountable public servant.

The integrated moral perspective can bind public administrators to a common public service mission and thereby overcome organizational specialization and fragmentation both in philosophical and functional terms—this, even though public administrators are not generally hired for their moral sophistication and courage. Thus, the integrated moral perspective engenders moral literacy and moral advocacy at different levels of the hierarchy. Since in the hierarchy there is equal moral authority and responsibility but unequal power and expertise, attention to the distribution and deployment of moral authority and responsibility is crucial. In this regard, the moral organization engages in continual moral deliberation and dialogue, just as the progressive organization engages in continual quality improvement.

The introduction of moral perspectives into organizations is to confront the technocratic norms and misguided utilitarianism that govern most organizations today. For example, the unified moral perspective recognizes the fiction of the deontology–teleology–virtue–intuitionism separation and the politics–administration dichotomy. It provides a moral basis for dissolving these artificial divisions by emphasizing the inherently moral nature of administrative activities. It embodies the true unity of each division and obviates any attempt to compartmentalize administrative responsibility. It necessitates integrated moral thought and integrated moral action.

Imagine a public administrator who believes that ethics is job-related, whose thoughts, decisions, and actions are shaped by the unified moral perspective presented in the last chapter. As an autonomous moral agent, how does such an administrator manage or even occasionally resolve the ethical conflicts and quandaries in the administrative environment? More precisely, how does such an administrator cope with the vulnerability problem associated with principal–agent relation? What is the basis for such an administrator's claim to a role in governance? What is such an administrator's understanding of organizations in terms of moral autonomy, conscience, and loyalty? These are the key questions that must be answered in the development of a theory of moral agency in public administration, and these are the questions to which our integrated moral perspective directly applies.

The integrated moral perspective involves the nexus between ends, means, and responsibility. From this vantage point, it is not meaningful to separate one element from the other two. Implicit in this perspective is the recognition that principle, purpose, and personality are inextricably intertwined. To speak of principle without reference to its anticipated or expected effects or to the individual acting on its behalf is to distort the essential unity of theory and practice. Autonomy, as the freedom to behave responsibly, implies purpose and consequence, embodied in the cognition and action of the morally conscious and competent individual. It by no means implies deference to authority or heteronomy, which, in fact, violates Kant's conception of autonomy. Jos (1990) captures the essence of this point when he notes that "[e]xercising autonomy is not freedom to interpret the moral good as one sees fit; it is exercising the sensitivity, understanding, and courage necessary to fully and independently consider obligations to clients, superiors, elected officials, the Constitution, and fundamental principles in the course of one's duties" (p. 244). Jos, however, fails to provide a systematic justification of autonomy as a critical component of administrative ethics.

Such a justification, as we have seen, is grounded especially in the second and third formulations of Kant's categorical imperative: Treat all rational beings as ends in themselves and not as means; respect the autonomy of rational beings to produce a "kingdom of ends." These formulations indicate a regard for individual sovereignty and dignity, rather than individual submission or obedience, and a recognition of the connection between ends and means. Philip Selznick (1992) captures this idea in his discussion of instrumental rationality in relation to both individuals and organizations. He suggests that instrumental rationality does not preclude moral agency, and that if it did, it would be difficult to treat individuals as moral agents. He notes that we are often involved in "projects that demand fidelity to purpose or to selected values," but that we "are also persons, and as such have moral capacities and responsibilities, which intrude as necessary into the realm of work, refashioning means and ends" (p. 240). Further, with reference to organizations, Selznick suggests that "the demands of rationality cannot be met if the full interplay of means and ends is neglected. A narrow view of rationality, uninformed by the continuum of means–ends, is the chief flaw in the view that organizations are necessarily amoral" (pp. 240–241). It seems clear, then, that a theory of moral agency in public administration fundamentally requires an awareness that agency, by definition, entails a morally grounded grasp of the end–means connection, supplemented by those personal qualities that we call character. Kass (1989) is correct in his contention that agency is crucial to a coherent theory of ethics in public administration and in his concern about the possibility of abuse in public sector principal–agent relations. Our aim here is to elaborate the agency–ethics theory linkage and to address the "potential for injustice" that Kass claims "increases in a number of ways when the power of the state is involved" (p. 952).

There is no longer any serious question concerning whether public administrators make evaluative decisions, although some theorists may question whether it is proper for administrators to be anything more than followers of orders from the public and its representatives. The question is not whether, as a matter of practice, administrators make evaluations, but whether they should. We are now in a position to answer that question from the standpoint of ethical theory. Three of the four ethical theories that we have discussed can be shown to answer positively. The fourth, intuitionism, is difficult to examine, as it is in many cases, because intuitions vary. Although we hold that people's intuitive judgments would favor the freedom of administrators to make ethical judgments, we will assume that the intuitions are uncertain on the matter.

The Kantian position appears to speak most clearly on this issue. The second formulation of the categorical imperative makes clear that people, as rational beings, are to be treated as autonomous ends-in-themselves. One of the most critical features of persons is their freedom to make moral choices. If they are deprived of that freedom, they are robots rather than people.

We may also see a Kantian defense of this freedom in the first formulation of the categorical imperative. Let us suppose that we rendered the maxim "Public administrators should never make evaluative decisions" a universal law. Under such a rule, public administrators would be virtually unable to function. The public administrator would then be in the absurd position of being barred, by the rules of his profession, from functioning for the public good, which is the natural aim of that profession.

But we should not therefore assume that Kant would give total license to public administrators to act in any way that they wish. We saw that they, as promoters of the public good, must be given autonomy. But their autonomy is to be used for the purpose of promoting that good, as best they can discern it and within the limits of their profession. Since the application of the first formulation of the categorical imperative depends upon the status of the individual as a professional, consistency requires that he or she remain true to the purpose and defining limits of the profession. One's status as a city planner, for example, warrants the autonomy necessary to function professionally, but that same status requires that she function within the norms of that profession.

One might object, however, that Kant's analysis seems contradictory on this issue. The autonomy of a public official, such as a city planner, is restricted by the demands of the profession and is, therefore, apparently less than one's autonomy as a person. Since the status of the professional is more restrictive than that of a person, there would appear to be a conflict between autonomy limited by professional duties and broader autonomy that one would have as a human being. But this apparent conflict dissolves when one fully understands the concept of autonomy. It is not unrestricted freedom or license. Autonomy is the freedom to act as a responsible human being. Its opposite, for Kant, is not slavery but heteronomy, the state of being controlled by one's desires. Autonomy is the freedom to choose and act morally. The responsible human being who functions within a specific profession will honor the restrictions that her profession places upon her. Thus, her professional duty becomes also her personal moral duty.

The teleological utilitarian would also favor providing the public administrator with the autonomy necessary to perform his or her duties. The fact that public administrators, by necessity, must make evaluative decisions is ample evidence that the happiness of the public would suffer if that power would be removed. As with Kant, however, the utilitarian would demand that the administrator's freedom be used for the public good rather than as a means of supporting one's own agenda.

There is also good reason from the standpoint of the character-based theorist for providing the public administrator with moral autonomy. To deprive her of it would remove her opportunity to express her character, develop it as one does with practice in any area of excellence, and provide an example for others to follow in developing their character. But as with the Kantian and the utilitarian, the character-based theorist would regard the autonomy positively only if it is used for morally praiseworthy behavior. If the public administrator behaves in a morally questionable manner, she would have used her freedom to set a poor public example for others and a bad precedent for herself.

We have argued that the integrated ethical perspective can help a public administrator to be both a democrat and a technocrat, that it comprehends the ethical and technical aspects of administrative responsibility, and that it offers ethical empowerment—an awareness of ethical unity and the confidence to act as a moral advocate and as a steward of the public trust. We believe that the integrated ethical perspective provides a framework from which practitioners can approach decisions and actions with a coherent moral point of view. On the practical level, this framework consists of asking four questions designed to promote ethical analysis and action in the context of the ends–means–character connection: (1) What principles are at stake in this situation? (2) What purposes should I try to achieve, and what are their likely consequences?

(3) What are the connections of these principles and purposes to my character? (4) How do I feel about it?

In our view, if a public administrator asks these questions in good faith and attempts to be consistent, then a foundation will be laid for taking a publicly justifiable position. Asking these questions, of course, will not guarantee moral consensus. Indeed, it is likely that differing assumptions, perceptions, priorities, and pressures will play on the participants in any decision. The integrated moral perspective does not eliminate contending interpretations of circumstances, relationships, and goals. But it does provide an ethical baseline grounded in human nature and the continua of the world, rather than artificial categories imposed to suit established systems of thought and structures of authority. The point, in any event, is to raise these questions with clarity and conviction, to recognize that segmenting policy or management issues into their components of principle, purpose, consequence, and judgment and acting on each separately is not to be realistic but to distort reality. In this regard, we argue that, whereas Frederickson's (1997) description of the administrative environment as unrelentingly teleological may contain some degree of truth, such a one-dimensional characterization is an inadequate reflection of administrative ethics. As Stewart (1984) has noted, most managers tend to synthesize teleology and deontology, rather than to rely exclusively on one or the other. Although this synthesis may not be systematic, reflective or complete, it does demonstrate the viability of grounding our integrated ethical perspective in established administrative practice, as well as conjoined theoretical principles. Thus, it is incumbent on administrators and scholars alike, as moral agents, to understand the fundamental philosophical and practical unity of their enterprise.

With respect to the vulnerability problem in principal–agent relations, we argue that our integrated ethical perspective would obviate or at least reduce the likelihood of abuse. An autonomous moral agent, genuinely operating from this perspective, would have sufficient moral clarity and conviction to avoid self-deception, deception of the principal, coercion, and collusion. Kass (1989) is correct in his claim that the special obligations between the agent and the principal, as well as the universal justice norm, mitigate vulnerability. We maintain that our integrated ethical perspective, shaped by the ends–means–virtue nexus, can strengthen the fiduciary and agent norms, which Kass contends help to alleviate the vulnerability problem. Moreover, the moral agent, grounded in the integrated ethical perspective, would find Kass's focus on the republic quite compatible in both philosophical and functional terms. Just as the basic association and process give coherence to the political system itself, the integrated ethical perspective gives moral coherence to the public administrator. The unity that characterizes the republic parallels the unity that characterizes moral agency.

Turning to the basis of the public administrator's claim to a place in governance, we have seen that neither expertise nor position alone provides sufficient justification if the claim is to be morally supportable. The autonomous agential role based on a claim of expertise or position is inherently suspect as a normative guide for the cultivation of public virtues. To propose that autonomous agency be based on claims to a role in governance animated by expertise or position is essentially to privilege teleology at the expense of deontology and virtue. While technical skill, ascriptive guardianship, and surrogate citizenship may be important ingredients in the administrator's role, their link to moral agency is not self-evident or automatic. Therefore, rather than simply assume that a place in governance based on expertise or position is a justifiable foundation for an autonomous agential role, we must delineate an administrative role in governance more closely aligned with the integrated ethical perspective.

The integrated ethical perspective predicates the public administrator's position as a moral agent on an understanding, indeed an internalization, of the philosophical and functional continua in ethical theory and practice. It maintains that the morally literate advocate draws no artificial or arbitrary lines between principle, purpose, and character. It rejects the notion that expertise can provide normative guidance in management and policy decisions, and it finds equally insupportable the attempt to derive agential legitimacy for public administrators from generalities such as commitment to the public interest, the common good, or the Constitution. While they are appropriate aspects of administrative ethics and behavior, they are reflections, rather than sources, of moral agency and autonomy.

The basis for a public administrator's role in governance must be the comprehensive moral point of view embodied in our integrated ethical perspective. Such a point of view can help to engender ethical clarity, conviction and sophistication, and can contribute to the moral legitimacy of an administrative role in governance as well as to the moral foundation for administrative commitment to the public interest, the common good, and the Constitution. The integrated ethical perspective systematizes and expands the existing administrative synthesis of deontology and teleology and provides a new understanding of the essential elements of moral agency. Just as deontology, teleology, and virtue implicate each other in theory, the moral agent embodies each of them in practice, as she strives to provide principled expertise as a steward of the public trust and the public interest.

What is the nature of the relationship between the moral agent and the public organization? How do autonomy, conscience, and loyalty figure into this relationship? First, the moral agent, operating from the integrated ethical perspective, appreciates the theoretical and functional complexity of organizations. Just as life is not one thing, as Cooper (1990) suggests, organizations are not one thing. Clearly, organizations exist on multiple planes, with significant variation in purposes, processes, and resources. Therefore, the moral agent has a textured, nuanced view of organizations, which includes their role as members of the moral order. The moral agent understands that organizations are involved in the articulation and achievement of values, that they consist of cultures, socialization, and patterns of behavior, and that they try to maintain their identity in a complex political environment. As Selznick (1992) notes, "a government agency may be a locus of commitment and value for its staff or for a special constituency, yet may be conceived and handled in quite narrowly instrumental terms by the larger system of which it is a part" (p. 233). Moreover, the moral agent is aware of institutionalization as the creation of social integration and commitments or, in Selznick's (1992) words, the infusion of "value beyond the technical requirements of the task at hand" (p. 233), and is also aware of the distinction between an organization and an institution. As Selznick suggests, an "organization is a special-purpose tool, a rational instrument engineered to do a job, a lean, no-nonsense system of consciously coordinated activities. An institution, on the other hand, is better understood as a product of social adaptation, largely unplanned, often a result of converging interests" (p. 233). He observes that a "given enterprise need not be solely either one or the other. On the contrary, most are complex mixtures of designed and adaptive problem-solving" (p. 233). Finally, the moral agent knows, like Selznick, that "institutionalization may be positive or negative," that it "depends on *what* is being institutionalized" (p. 234). As he points out, "[w]e cannot determine the moral worth of an institution without knowing its character and what ends it serves" (p. 234).

In light of these organizational complexities, the moral agent resists demonizing organizations as the sources of all evil or repression. The moral agent recognizes, as Selznick (1992) notes, that "organizational imperatives often lead to immoral outcomes—deception, corruption, exploitation, domination" (p. 240); but there is also a recognition that "such outcomes are variable" and that the "variability shows that rational systems need not be amoral" (p. 240). Again, the moral agent, like Selznick, appreciates the interplay of means and ends.

The moral agent, as an autonomous and accountable steward, also appreciates both the Kantian ideal of moral autonomy and the existentialist association of autonomy with actual experience. As Selznick says, "[t]o be truly autonomous is to act, not in the light of principle alone, even self-determined principle, but on the basis of concrete judgments regarding moral outcomes. There cannot be genuine freedom of moral decision when choices are predetermined by abstract rules. Authentic existence is the result of engagement as well as principle" (pp. 70–71). Selznick refers to Martin Buber's "I–Thou" as "the paradigm of authentic, self-affirming engagement" (p. 71). It upholds "a Kantian ideal, the principle of respect for all persons as ends in themselves, but with far more awareness of the struggle entailed and of the conditions that must be fulfilled" (p. 71). The moral agent, imbued with the integrated ethical perspective, embodies this central connection between principle, purpose, and character in the continuing process of trying to strike a balance between conscience, loyalty, and autonomous choice.

The Skokie Case

Although we cited Gerald Pops (1994) as generally sharing our belief that teleology and deontology form a unity, he touches on that unity only superficially and treats virtue only in passing. Furthermore, he appears to confuse teleology with egoism. To demonstrate our differences with him and to show how our theory of unity applies in practice, we examine his analysis of the well-known case of the Skokie, Illinois, Nazi demonstration. First, we summarize the case according to Pops; second, we assess his position; and third, we approach the case from the perspective of our integrated model. In the process, we hope to highlight the model's greater clarity, consistency, and applicability to administrative practice.

The case involves a request from a group of Nazis for a parade permit from the town of Skokie, Illinois. Pops argues that the conflict in this case concerns the deontological stance—protection of the First Amendment—versus the sensibilities of the many Holocaust survivors who are residents of Skokie. Presumably, their sensibilities represent the teleological stance, although Pops is not clear on this point. In any event, while the law is clear and the city may not discriminate in its issuing parade permits based on the participants' beliefs, Pops maintains that practical consequences should dissuade the town manager from granting the permit. He offers three reasons: (1) The town manager wishes to serve the citizens of a community which does not include Nazis; (2) the town manager thinks that the Nazis can express themselves elsewhere; (3) the town manager wishes to keep his job and denying the permit makes him a local hero and makes the courts the villains.

Yet, Pops continues, "[a] public administrator must be concerned with the legitimacy of her actions as well as with outcomes. Thus, the administrator will often speak the language of deontological ethics but search for devices to justify favoring a good result where it is seen to conflict with principle" (p. 162). This might involve arguing ethical relativism; playing the legal card, which might entail obfuscation or substituting "not doing anything illegal for being ethical"; playing the professional card, which might mean deferring to experts; or seeking the counsel of a few and avoiding written communications and public forums. Nonetheless, Pops expresses concern about teleological reasoning, suggesting that, at least in Machiavellian form, it could lead to organizational mediocrity, resistance to change, and system stability rather than excellence. He concludes with a call for ethical inclusiveness in which he points to the dangers for public administration of the unrestrained use of teleological ethics and asserts that a theory of ethics truly concerned with consequences must balance utility, rights, justice, and self-interest.

Pops's position can be faulted on technical, moral, and practical grounds. First, he mistakes egoism for the sum total of teleology. While it is true, as noted earlier, that egoism is a form of teleology, it is by no means the dominant expression of the teleological perspective. In fairness, however, we must note that Pops's error is not only common but often extends as well to utilitarianism, the dominant teleological perspective. Nevertheless, this distortion of teleology leads Pops to characterize it as especially susceptible to Machiavellian machinations, which can result in all manner of organizational dysfunction and personal trauma. Utilitarianism, contrary to popular public administration perception, is not the moral equivalent of cost–benefit analysis or unbridled self-interest.

On moral grounds, Pops is vulnerable on a number of counts. Consider his advice to the town manager. First, he suggests that the town manager should deny the parade permit because Skokie's population does not include Nazis. This is clearly a *non sequitur,* which also has serious implications. Suppose, for example, that members of the Bahai faith wished to march in Skokie and that no Bahai lived in the community. For the sake of consistency, would Pops advise the town manager to deny them a parade permit? Or, perhaps, even more to the point, suppose that Jews requested a parade permit from a city with no Jews. Would Pops feel it appropriate for their request to be denied on demographic grounds? Clearly, Pops's circumscribed view of the basis for allowing free expression of noxious beliefs does not meet even elementary standards of logic or fairness.

Pops's second piece of advice—Nazis can express themselves elsewhere—bespeaks a kind of NIMBY logic. It is not only irrelevant but is also a striking interpretation of the scope of administrative responsibility. Are public administrators to implement the law based on convenience and their perception or hope that it can be implemented in another jurisdiction with less controversy?

Pops's third and final piece of advice to the town manager—deny the permit, knowing the case will go to court, and thereby keep your job—is perhaps the most egregious. Once again, it involves the worst form of teleological reasoning: egoism. It is not utilitarianism but simply self-interest, which condones the artful management of the very Holocaust survivors whom the town manager is purportedly trying to protect. The town manager is encouraged to manipulate and maneuver in order to appear as a hero to the community's Jewish residents and to cast the courts as the villain. It treats those residents as means, not ends, as mere instruments to suit the purposes of the town manager, and it discounts their capacity to penetrate the deception and hold the town manager accountable.

Finally, on practical grounds, Pops's advice is also flawed. For example, one of the unmentioned possible, even likely, consequences of denying the parade permit is a lawsuit. Indeed, that likelihood is implicit in the town manager's stratagem to cast himself as the hero and the courts as the villain. The community, therefore, will incur legal expenses in what is implicitly a losing cause. Moreover, one must wonder how, in the long run, Pops's advice to the town manager can be considered a practical move toward a balance of utility, rights, justice, and self-interest. On the contrary, it may well be seen as nothing more than a transparent, illegitimate, self-serving ploy, which eventually will be discovered to the chagrin, or worse, of the town manager.

We now come to the integrated ethical approach and its theoretical, moral, and practical superiority over dichotomous deontological and teleological thinking. How would a public administrator proceeding from our unified perspective resolve the Skokie dilemma? First, we believe that Stewart (1984) is correct when she observes that deontology and teleology are synthesized in practice. Although this practical synthesis may be unreflexive and unsystematic, it nonetheless can move us toward the realization that we cannot speak, for example, of obligation or responsibility from a partial or truncated point of view. Indeed, unlike Pops, a practitioner operating from a unified perspective would not envisage unrestrained teleological thinking, nor would she imagine unrestrained deontological thinking. Neither is possible, given the conceptual and practical nexus connecting them to each other and to virtue.

The holistic practitioner, so to speak, would be aware that in the teleological tradition, decisions are judged by their consequences, depending on the results to be maximized, but also would ask where the desirability of consequences originates. Such a practitioner also would recognize that the deontologist's goal is not simply to preserve the purity of principle but to achieve consequences maximally consistent with principle. Indeed, one might argue that happiness—a utilitarian goal—will be increased by observing deontological principles. For example, we contend that both the public interest and justice embody the spirit of our unity of deontology, teleology, and character theory. Each simultaneously is a value to seek and a value to effect. Or to put it in another way, the fusion of deontology, teleology, and character theory is predicated on three presuppositions, namely, that deontology presupposes a moral consequence, teleology presupposes a moral end, and that character is the connecting link. Like theory and practice or facts and values, they are philosophically and practically indissoluble.

Under the circumstances, therefore, our administrator would be incapable, either ethically or intellectually, of considering the manipulation of Jewish Skokie residents, particularly on the basis of self-interest or careerism. The moral bankruptcy of such action would be painfully obvious. Politically, the framework within which our administrator thinks and decides would make it clear that Pops's advice is not only immoral but highly impractical. Specifically, to use administrative discretion to deny constitutional protection to the Nazis because of the offended sensibilities of certain constituents would not enhance one's credibility as a responsible decision maker. In this particular case, at the very least, our administrator would consult with the town council, the legal counsel, and colleagues, in order to determine as far as possible whether a clear and present danger exists as well as the source of that danger. In any event, unilateral decision making based on the reasons offered by Pops would be singularly inappropriate on both the moral and political level.

The Skokie example allows us also to recognize an important consequence of the unity of deontology, teleology, and character. Public administrators who consider their positions to be only instruments of a state or agency tend to think of themselves as outside of the moral environment. They see themselves as means to ends that they are not to question, while following rules that are unwelcome obstacles in pursuit of the assigned goals. They are, they would suppose, purely teleological and thus non-moral. Yet, not only is this belief mistaken, but the Skokie case decisively refutes it. If deontology, teleology, and character cannot be separated, then everyone is necessarily and always a moral agent.

Bureaucratic Ethos and Democratic Ethos

We now consider two major questions: (1) the reconciliation of the bureaucratic ethos with the democratic ethos; and (2) the reconciliation of bureaucracy with democracy. We show, first, that the bureaucratic ethos and the democratic ethos represent a false dichotomy, which perpetuates fragmented administrative thought and action. Second, we show that the bureaucratic ethos and democratic ethos, joined by character, can be unified by the application of our integrated ethical perspective. With regard to the bureaucracy–democracy dilemma, we propose a reconciliation based on a reconceptualization of principal–agent relations. We show, in particular, that the integrated ethical perspective can contribute to the resolution of this dilemma through its formulation of moral agency. We argue that moral agency not only provides philosophical grounding for reconciling bureaucracy with democracy but is also central to the practical problems faced by administrators, elected officials, and citizens in the overall governance process.

With respect to the reconciliation of the bureaucratic ethos and democratic ethos, we focus on the work of Pugh (1991), who claims that the bureaucratic ethos and democratic ethos constitute "the principal frameworks for approaching public management ethics" (p. 10). Pugh's essay is the centerpiece of our discussion, since it represents the position held by a number of public administration scholars, with the possible exception of Stewart (1984) who, as we noted earlier, argues that administrators tend to synthesize deontology and teleology in actual practice. Pugh argues that the bureaucratic ethos is characterized by efficiency, efficacy, expertise, loyalty, and accountability, while the democratic ethos is characterized by regime values, citizenship, public interest, and social equity. The bureaucratic ethos is associated with Weberian bureaucracy, the politics–administration dichotomy, scientific management, and rationalism. The democratic ethos, on the other hand, is associated with constitutional values as "general guides to moral reasoning in public administration" (p. 15), an informed and active citizenry, a public interest characterized by rational thought, disinterestedness, benevolence, and fairness or justice. "Bureaucratic ethos," according to Pugh, "is teleological, employs instrumental rationality, and is predicated on the values of capitalism and a market society. Democratic ethos, in contrast, is deontological, is based on substantive rationality, and emanates from classical values of the state and higher law" (p. 26). Finally, Pugh maintains that the bureaucratic ethos and democratic ethos are not only *not* complementary to each other but are alternatives or even threats to each other. To buttress his point, he cites Paul Appleby (1952) who, in *Morality and Administration in Democratic Government,* argued that "[t]here is no single problem in public administration of moment equal to the reconciliation of the increasing dependence upon [bureaucratic] experts with an enduring democratic reality" (p. 145). Nonetheless, Pugh contends that even though public administration "has claimed to reject the politics/administration dichotomy—replacing its emphasis on the word *administration* with an emphasis on the word *public*—the operational values have remained bureaucratic" (p. 26). In Pugh's estimation, "as long as the field's assumptions are shaped by bureaucratic ethos the politics we speak of will not be democratic" (pp. 26–27). Indeed, he notes that even Max Weber recognized that policy must be considered on both technical and normative grounds in the context of general cultural values.

Given the unity of deontology, teleology, and character demonstrated in chapter 4, the putative dichotomy between the bureaucratic ethos and democratic ethos easily dissolves. They are, in fact, two sides of the same coin. Deontology, as one aspect of objective ethics, includes both intentionality and concern about consequences consistent with principle, as well as responsibility and accountability. Teleology, a second element of objective ethics, is clearly not driven by egoism or unprincipled pleasure but, rather, by the achievement of ends conducive to general happiness. Thus, there is no logical basis for believing that the values of either ethos are mutually exclusive of the other. It is quite likely that a public administrator, with the requisite character, can be an efficient, loyal, and accountable expert who, at the same time, subscribes to constitutional principles and strives to serve the public interest. Contrary to Pugh's claim that the bureaucratic ethos and the democratic ethos are alternatives, at best, or antagonists, at worst, they are, in combination with virtue, inseparable ingredients in our moral nature. Furthermore, if public administration's assumptions continue to be shaped by the bureaucratic ethos, in spite of the purported rejection of the politics–administration dichotomy, then it is because of an incomplete understanding of principle, purpose, and practice, rather than an intrinsic division of deontology, teleology, and character. Management and policy issues can be approached simultaneously on both technical and normative grounds, as Weber argued, if their inherent unity is acknowledged and accepted.

Besides its misinterpretation of deontology and teleology, as well as its exclusion of virtue, Pugh's discussion is problematic on additional grounds. For example, he suggests that "[t]he content values of bureaucratic ethos are chiefly contained in five pervasive concepts: efficiency, efficacy, expertise, loyalty, and accountability" (p. 10). If efficiency, efficacy, expertise, loyalty, and accountability are concepts, then what are the values themselves? We suggest that they are traditional democratic values grounded in our moral and philosophical unity. Moreover, for purposes of clarification, we note that, in his comments on the methodology of the bureaucratic ethos and the democratic ethos, Pugh makes a common error and continues the ambiguity in his discussion. He describes the methodology of the democratic ethos as deductive or "reasoning from a general truth to a particular instance of that truth" (p. 17) when, in fact, deductive reasoning refers to a process in which a conclusion drawn from a set of premises does not go beyond the information in the premises themselves. This is in contrast to inductive reasoning, which refers to drawing a conclusion that does go beyond the information in the premises presented, although Pugh does not ascribe inductive reasoning to the bureaucratic ethos. Instead, in reference to its methodology, he claims that "content values are assessed against established rational goals and objectives using instrumentalism and utilitarianism as the criteria for action" (pp. 13–14). Again, Pugh's assertion is striking in its ambiguity and misrepresentation of utilitarianism. We must ask about the meaning of values being assessed against rational goals and objectives and about instrumentalism and utilitarianism being the assessment tools. Which values does he have in mind? We do not know if he is referring to efficiency, efficacy, expertise, loyalty, and accountability since earlier he said that these are concepts that contain the values of the bureaucratic ethos. Second, what, precisely, is the purpose of juxtaposing values with rational goals and objectives, instrumentalism and utilitarianism? Presumably, it is to imply technical predominance over value-based motives and concerns. As we have shown, however, to associate utilitarianism with valueless instrumentalism is very much mistaken.

Despite its conceptual and analytical flaws, Pugh's essay is valuable in two respects. First, he notes the superficial attention paid in administrative ethics courses and administrative settings to the bureaucratic ethos and democratic ethos as means to approach ethical problems. Citing Hejka-Ekins (1988), Pugh points out that there is little depth in understanding or use of either ethos, which results in confusion in both the classroom and the workplace. According to Pugh, an important deficiency in this regard is that "[s]tudents not only remain ignorant of the historical, sociological, and ideological meanings of these frameworks but also appear to be left unaware of how differently these approaches frame reality. . . ." (p. 25). Although we agree with the essentials of Pugh's position, we believe that his treatment of the bureaucratic ethos and democratic ethos suffers from the same deficiency. At the same time, however, his concern with the substance of these frameworks, rather than pedagogy, is a step in the right direction. The second respect in which Pugh's discussion is valuable is his call for additional work "to ferret out the historical, sociological, and ideological differences between the two frameworks" (p. 27). Clearly, interdisciplinary approaches to these issues would represent an advance in both theory and practice. In this connection, we would add philosophy to Pugh's list of social science disciplines, particularly applied ethics, as a crucial component in mapping the moral terrain of public administration. As Pugh says, "the issue of ethics for public administration, and by extension public management, is inherently a broader issue of political theory and the role of the administrative state in contemporary society . . . to engage ethics is to engage our theory of politics" (p. 30).

We focused on Pugh's position because it is representative of the dichotomous ethical thinking among leading public administration theorists. It presumes a distinction between deontology and teleology, which we have shown is inaccurate on moral as well as philosophical grounds. Worse, it validates the fragmentation of moral thought among practitioners whose resultant decisions and actions suffer from moral incoherence and ambiguity. Like deontology, teleology, and virtue, the bureaucratic ethos and democratic ethos are not separate entities. Rather, they constitute a single indissoluble unit, which can help to provide public administrators with the clarity and coherence required to act as moral agents.

Bureaucracy and Democracy

Shifting from the bureaucratic ethos–democratic ethos issue to the bureaucracy–democracy dilemma reveals the power and potential of moral agency as a medium of reconciliation. A long-standing issue predicated on the presumption of conflicting values, the bureaucracy–democracy dilemma is the bureaucratic ethos–democratic ethos issue writ large. As we will show in our review of relevant literature, the bureaucracy–democracy dilemma reflects the same kind of dichotomous thinking demonstrated on the level of the bureaucratic ethos and the democratic ethos. Principle and purpose are presented as either–or choices, with no recognition of their underlying unity. Therefore, we argue that the application of our integrated ethical perspective, as well as a reconceptualization of principal–agent relations, can contribute to a resolution of this dilemma and lead to a new understanding in both electoral institutions, to use Kenneth Meier's (1997) term, and administrative organizations. This understanding, in turn, would be inextricably linked to a redefinition of governance, which in Meier's view is central to the problems in American government (Meier, 1997). In fact, Meier maintains that, given the declining performance of electoral institutions, what is needed is "a normative orientation, with public administration concerned with how governance should be structured and operated rather than just how the bureaucracy should implement public policy" (p. 197). We contend that moral agency, enunciated as a comprehensive objective ethics, can be integral to the development of such an orientation.

Our discussion of the bureaucracy–democracy dilemma and principal–agent relations is most directly informed by the work of Douglas Yates (1982), Eva Etzioni-Halevy (1983), Judith E. Gruber (1987), B. Dan Wood and Richard W. Waterman (1994), Kenneth J. Meier (1997), and Louis C. Gawthrop (1997). In combination, these scholars frame the key questions around which a theory of moral agency in public administration can be formulated. We begin with Yates (1982), who suggests that American government has increasingly become what he calls a bureaucratic democracy. Democratic decision making takes place more and more in bureaucracies. The models that Yates proposes to encapsulate this contention are pluralist democracy and administrative efficiency, and he says that it makes sense "to assert that government should be both democratic and efficient. The problem is that the particular American understanding of democracy and administrative efficiency causes the two objectives to come sharply into conflict" (p. 9). Our claim, in this regard, is that our integrated objective ethics makes it possible, on the moral as well as the practical level, to assert both democracy and efficiency in American government without the conflict caused by our present understanding.

After listing the trade-offs between pluralist democracy and administrative efficiency, including decentralization versus centralization, dispersion versus concentration of power, and allocation of power to citizens and politicians versus experts and bureaucrats, Yates argues that it is possible to imagine a political system in which power is given both to citizens and politicians, on the one hand, and to experts and bureaucrats, on the other. He claims that the critical question is which group ultimately gains an advantage in the balance of power. He also believes it is possible to imagine a political order in which individual preferences and technical rationality are both given strong weight but suggests that there comes a point when one must choose between the two criteria. To illustrate, Yates provides what he calls a "caricatured example" in which one can build a highway either along a straight line favored by engineers or according to adjustments supported by affected neighborhoods. But one cannot do both (p. 33). In any case, according to Yates, the central question concerning the conflict between the pluralist and efficiency models is whether to rely on the judgment and preferences of political actors or the findings of policy analysts. We suggest that this dichotomy is simplistic, since it pits politics, professional knowledge, and management against each other, takes a superficial view of utilitarianism, and fails to make explicit the articulation and adjudication of values and principles in the governance process.

Yates also asks whether the pluralist democracy and administrative efficiency models produce the results for which they are designed. He notes the continuing debate over interest groups, for example, and whether they are good for democracy; refers to the critiques of Theodore Lowi, Charles Lindblom, and others; and remarks on the view that single-issue politics is dominant. With respect to the administrative efficiency model, Yates adverts to both the defenders and critics of the model, noting that defenders point to the professional non-political military and space program, the lack of corruption among civil servants, and the crucial role of experts in such agencies as the Council of Economic Advisors, the National Security Council, and the Office of Management and Budget. Critics, on the other hand, see bureaucratic policy making as rigid, with professionalism as a barrier between citizens and experts, who have failed to solve the pressing problems in several policy areas such as energy and the economy. Finally, in this regard, Yates points to a third position in which there is no necessary conflict between democracy and efficiency. Lindblom, for example, argues that a system based on bargaining and mutual adjustment can be both democratic and efficient, and Norton Long contends that bureaucracy can serve the values of administrative efficiency while still sustaining democratic values such as group representation.

Yates discusses the conscientious bureaucrat who would defend himself against complaints and criticisms of bureaucracy by invoking his allegiance to administrative process values. The bureaucrat would argue that, while bureaucracy is not perfect, citizens and elected officials are protected against bureaucratic misjudgments and other suspect behaviors because bureaucrats are faithful to the administrative process values of accessibility, accountability, participation, responsiveness, and responsibility. Fidelity to these process values ensures that bureaucrats are performing democratically and efficiently. In Yates's judgment, although this defense is somewhat plausible, adherence to administrative process values may be misleading. Since their scope and meaning vary, they may be defined and applied in ways that imply different results for citizens and elected officials. Moreover, Yates believes it is worrisome when bureaucrats, especially at the lower levels, make valuative decisions on their own. On democratic grounds, this means that public decisions are made by officials who are either beyond the control of citizens or are loosely controlled, at best. On efficiency grounds, it undermines the norms of central executive leadership, hierarchical authority, and bureaucratic neutrality.

Yates concludes his analysis of the bureaucracy–democracy dilemma by first recommending open, public accounting of the valuative basis of decisions on significant policy issues. In his view, this accounting for decisions constitutes substantive responsibility. At the same time, however, Yates realizes that the meaning of "significant" in this connection is problematic, and he therefore suggests two criteria as guidelines: (1) A policy merits public accounting when it is either a non-routine new initiative or a marked departure from past practice; and (2) a policy merits public accounting when it attempts to apply a major social value such as equality, equal opportunity, personal liberty, or the public interest. We note in passing that Yates does not consider the forum, format, skill, or methodology for a public accounting of decisions and policies, and we suggest that these questions would have to be addressed by any public organization contemplating such a move.

Yates also offers several strategies for accommodating democracy and efficiency, the key step in which is revision of the norms of the administrative efficiency model. The critical revision is the alignment of our conception of the public manager's job with the actual bureaucratic environment, which is intensely political, fragmented, and value-laden. Yates argues that, while the two models do not converge into dissolution, neither do bureaucratic problems divide dichotomously into the proprietary concerns of each. Thus, it is logically possible that remedies to such problems will satisfy the norms of both pluralist democracy and administrative efficiency. Specifically, Yates's suggestions include: strong, centralized executive leadership, long-range planning and competitive budgeting, mini-cabinets, an executive secretariat, and an office of public service, which would have three major functions: (1) to address the problem that citizens and public officials often do not know what a bureaucracy actually does; (2) to increase the capacity for ombudsman-style activity; and (3) to create citizen advocates to represent interests that would otherwise be either weakly represented or entirely ignored.

According to Eva Etzioni-Halevy (1983), the role of bureaucracy in a democracy is problematic because it is one of the areas in which the democratic rules of the game are ill-defined, ambiguous, self-contradictory, and controversial. Bureaucracy generates a dilemma for democracy as it becomes more independent and powerful, posing a threat to the democratic political structure and to democratically elected politicians. Yet, an independent and powerful bureaucracy is also necessary for prevention of political corruption and for safeguarding proper democratic procedures. "Bureaucracy is thus a threat to, but also indispensable for, democracy" (p. 87).

Etzioni-Halevy (1983) also argues that self-contradictory democratic rules place bureaucracy in a double bind. Bureaucracy is expected to be both independent and subservient, both responsible for its own actions and subject to what she calls ministerial responsibility, both politicized and non-politicized at the same time. These dilemmas exacerbate strains and power struggles on the political scene. Moreover, as a potential threat to democracy, bureaucracy, according to Etzioni-Halevy, "may serve as a tool for the enhancement and greater efficacy of state domination, and in some cases of state repression" (p. 90). For example, she refers to concerns over information, secrecy, and privacy, and contends that bureaucracy has increasingly gained the potential of encroaching not only on individual privacy but also on autonomy and liberty—immunities which are the essence of democracy.

Why, then, is bureaucracy necessary for democracy? Etzioni-Halevy answers that the modern state is in charge of allocating enormous resources; for democratic procedures to work properly, it needs an organization that will carry out this function on a nonpartisan basis. This nonpartisan basis may consist of need, entitlement, or anything other than the potential or actual political support of the recipient for the donor and his party. Appointed bureaucrats, free from political pressure, can allocate resources by nonpartisan criteria. Without such an organization, there would be bribery and corruption; politicians would vie for office not on the basis of their policies or images, but on the basis of the resources they can marshal and deploy for their supporters' benefit. Thus, although bureaucracy may pose a threat to democracy owing to its exemption from political control and democratic accountability, such exemption is necessary to prevent the disruption of the democratic process itself.

Judith E. Gruber (1987) focuses on democratic control of bureaucracy, which she argues is difficult to achieve and which has multiple meanings. Control has many facets, including values, means, costs, extent, and impact. It also concerns our beliefs about democracy and the capability of citizens and elected officials compared to bureaucrats with their expertise and capacity for resistance. Controllers, in Gruber's view, must see control as a strategic problem of creating and marshaling resources. One strategy is to use formal authority to force bureaucrats to share their resources, especially information, with would-be controllers and to demystify bureaucratic processes (for example, the implementation of sunshine laws). According to Gruber, however, a claim by controllers to democratic authority is not a potent resource if bureaucrats see control as threatening other values. Successful controls, instead, are often those that can be aligned with bureaucrats' conceptions of their self-interest. For example, Gruber suggests that controllers parlay the resources that they command and that bureaucrats seek bureaucratic acceptance of control. Such resources include funding, information, access to political leaders, and cooperation.

Essentially, then, Gruber conceives of control as exchange. Central to this exchange is the creation of resources and the development of arenas for their strategic use. Although designing control mechanisms to coincide with bureaucrats' perceptions of their own interests may appear to violate the premises upon which the need for control is based, it also recognizes bureaucratic resistance and resources. It recognizes as well that "short of a fundamental change in the division of labor in democratic societies that eliminates the very existence of delegated authority, bureaucrats will have these resources and will be in a position to resist controls they do not find acceptable" (p. 213). Gruber concludes by observing that "[t]he road to successful control lies in understanding both the democratic and bureaucratic sides of the problem and carefully crafting efforts so that neither democratic norms nor bureaucratic facts are denied" (p. 214).

B. Dan Wood and Richard W. Waterman (1994) address a number of the issues considered by the other scholars cited here. For example, they note the increasing complexity, interdependence, and technical nature of society and the corresponding reliance of legislative bodies on bureaucracies owing to bureaucratic expertise. They point out that the principles of separation of powers and checks and balances are violated when bureaucracy performs all three governmental functions, when it makes and executes policy and adjudicates disputes resulting from its policy execution. They refer to a number of potential dangers of bureaucratic dominance in the policy process, such as auditing private records, seizing private property, compelling testimony, imposing fines and fees without hearings, collecting taxes, issuing licenses, making rules, and adjudicating controversies involving itself. Thus, their discussion recognizes the critical questions or normative controversies, which they argue have evolved from the politics–administration dichotomy. They note three questions in particular: First, how much policy-making authority should Congress delegate to the bureaucracy? Second, is a purely top-down model of political–bureaucratic relations appropriate? Third, what are the respective roles of Congress and the president in directing administrative policy making? By implication, these questions, of course, apply to state and local government as well.

In the context of these three questions, Wood and Waterman (1994) propose principal–agent theory or agency theory as a promising approach to the bureaucracy–democracy dilemma. Noting the emergence of agency theory in the early 1980s as a framework for describing political–bureaucratic relations, Wood and Waterman argue it explicitly assumes that elected officials or principals have political incentives to control bureaucrats or agents. Like the politics–administration dichotomy, agency theory posits that the relationship between principals and agents is hierarchical. Over time, however, disjunctures develop between their respective interests. For example, coalitions change from those that existed when legislative institutions first adopted the policies; bureaucracies develop separate interests; and politicians seek to alter established policy toward their preferred objectives, which may not be the same as those of the original legislation or past coalitions. In any event, agency theory posits a dynamic interactive process between principals and agents that evolves through time.

Wood and Waterman (1994) also maintain that shirking occurs from demands for stability or change by current officials or past statutory mandates, and they suggest that the key question for agency theory, therefore, is how politicians vested with contemporaneous legitimacy can overcome uncertainties and the bureaucratic tendency to shirk. At the heart of this question is the information asymmetry between the principal and the agent, as well as bureaucratic uncertainty about the politician's intentions. To support their claim, Wood and Waterman quote Charles Perrow's (1986) *Complex Organizations:* "The principal–agent model is fraught with the problems of cheating, limited information, and bounded rationality in general" (p. 224). This description, of course, is reminiscent of the observations by Kass. As an example of a process involving the elements of agency theory (i.e., cheating, deception, limited information, and bounded rationality), Wood and Waterman cite budgeting. Finally, they note two other elements relevant to agency theory: moral hazard and adverse selection. Moral hazard concerns the actions of economic agents who maximize their own utility to the detriment of others in situations where they do not bear the full consequences of their actions because of uncertainty and incomplete constraints. Adverse selection derives from what Wood and Waterman call the "nonobservability" of the information, beliefs, and values on which contractual decisions are based. It occurs when the principal makes a mistake in selecting the agent.

Wood and Waterman (1994) then turn to the question of how agency theory contributes to the goal of controlling the bureaucracy. "The answer is that control is possible because elected principals create bureaucracies" (p. 24). According to Wood and Waterman, bureaucracies are designed with various incentive structures to facilitate effective control, and political principals continually monitor the activities of their bureaucratic agents. When bureaucracies stray from principals' preferences, policy makers can apply sanctions or rewards to bring agents back into line. Agency theory posits that well-informed central decision makers systematically mold the preferences of bureaucratic agents through time. Or to put it in another way, agency theory claims that overhead democracy is possible in the United States. While agency theory differs from much existing literature in its emphasis on hierarchy, its assumptions about the role of the bureaucratic agent are not very different from those of earlier bureaucratic theory. Both conceptualize the bureaucracy as resistant to change. The major difference is agency theory's emphasis on a more active role for political principals. In contrast to iron triangle and capture theories, for example, agency theory posits that elected principals are active participants with firmly held policy preferences.

Moving to policy monitoring, in particular, Wood and Waterman (1994) suggest that the goal in agency relationship is to derive more effective and less costly monitoring capabilities to offset the information asymmetries that naturally exist between principals and agents. In this regard, they adapt John W. Pratt and Richard J. Zeckhauser's seven features of monitoring. Although Pratt and Zeckhauser's description of monitoring refers to the private sector, Wood and Waterman argue that it is relevant to the public sector as well. In any event, the seven features focus on such variables as the cost of monitoring as a factor in the quantity or quality of monitoring; the impact on the agency of divergent principal and agent interests or values; the effect of bad behavior on agency reputation and stability; the importance of long-term relationships that reduce the need for monitoring; and the common interest of the principal and the agent in producing outcomes with less monitoring cost.

In the context of these features, Wood and Waterman cite the contention that existing monitoring capabilities, such as congressional hearings, are largely ineffective because they involve a considerable political cost. The political payoff is far greater from campaigning, fund raising, speeches, and constituent service. Therefore, if the political costs of oversight can be reduced, effective oversight of the bureaucracy is more likely to occur. Furthermore, with respect to the question how to devise a low-cost, effective monitoring capacity, Wood and Waterman suggest that the focus should be on a particular output or series of outputs or outcomes, instead of everything in which a bureaucracy is involved. In addition, one of the most significant elements in Pratt and Zeckhauser's seven features of monitoring concerns the natural constraints on the behavior of bureaucratic agents. They are aware that their reputations can be severely damaged if they are found to have misled political principals. "Thus," Wood and Waterman argue, "even though there may be a natural tendency toward shirking, the possible short-term gains from providing misleading information to a principal must be weighed against the possibility of long-term damage to an agent's reputation" (p. 134). Indeed, they believe that a monitoring system capable of providing objective information on agency activities can enhance that agency's reputation and provide evidence for increased regulatory authority or appropriations. Finally, Wood and Waterman contend that a common interest between principals and agents can be derived if the goal of oversight is not one-sided, that is, if the focus of monitoring is not solely on the bureaucratic agent. If monitoring is extended to the principal, then a common interest is more likely to be achieved.

Wood and Waterman (1994) argue that bureaucracies represent both historical and contemporaneous coalitions; therefore, they perform an integrative function for American democracy. They blend demands from the past and present to produce a policy at a consistent level, and political principals share this responsibility with bureaucracy for assuring that the bureaucratic state is consistent with democracy and constitutional principles. Wood and Waterman recommend, in this connection, a return to a two-tiered principal–agent hierarchy established by the Constitution. Congress should assume the primary responsibility for policy making, and the president should assume the primary responsibility for administration. Since the two most important tools for controlling the bureaucracy are political appointment and the budget, Congress should focus on policy in its confirmation of nominees. Moreover, the congressional budget should be the primary working document. The Congressional Budget Office should be expanded, and bureaucracies should submit their budgets to the CBO rather than the Office of Management and Budget to ensure congruence with congressional policy. Most important, Congress should also strengthen its capacity for monitoring the executive branch, particularly by increasing the authority of the General Accounting Office. Presumably, principal–agent relations at the state and local level would encompass parallel reforms.

In the Waldo Symposium published in *Public Administration Review* (May/June 1997), Kenneth J. Meier argues that the bureaucracy problem is actually a governance problem, by which he means that electoral institutions, rather than administrative institutions or bureaucracy, are the source of our difficulty (Meier, 1997). Meier explains that he uses the term "electoral institutions" rather than political institutions to refer to Congress and the presidency because he believes that bureaucracy is also a political institution. In his view, "[t]he fundamental problem of governance that has generated the continual state of crisis in political bureaucratic relationships is that the electoral branches of government have failed as deliberative institutions; they have not resolved conflict in a reasoned manner" (p. 196). Meier maintains, moreover, that bureaucratic–democratic relations have "swung too far in the direction of democracy" and that "[t]he solution to the governance problem in the United States is to have more bureaucracy and less democracy" (p. 196).

Recognizing that this argument for less democracy implies fundamental change, Meier offers several suggestions to initiate the debate, including redesigning our political system to resolve rather than exacerbate conflict; lengthening the time for policy making, which means longer terms for elected officials; restricting and perhaps even eliminating political appointees, whom he sees as "a layer of incompetence between elected officials and the career bureaucracy"; assessing the trend toward privatization; extending the merit system to the institutionalized presidency; replacing the current public philosophy of neoclassical economics and its sole value of efficiency with a public philosophy that unites rather than divides and that values public service; and reorienting our education programs from training entry-level civil servants to training policy makers (p. 197).

Louis C. Gawthrop's (1997) contribution to the Waldo Symposium concerns the hypocrisy that he and Dwight Waldo believe results from the fusion of democracy and bureaucracy. He argues that "[t]he demand of adapting the prevailing canons of management to the intrinsic values of democracy create a professional environment wherein the art of pretense, the methods of acting or playing a role—indeed, of wearing a mask—become virtual prerequisites for a successful career" (p. 205). Gawthrop quotes Waldo who argued: "Hypocrisy enters because the 'dialectic' between democracy and bureaucracy offers extraordinary opportunities for confusion and self-delusion and invites self-serving opinions" (p. 205), and then suggests that "[o]ne reason for confusion and delusion is that the engines of democracy and bureaucracy run on different tracks, leaving from different stations and heading for different destinations" (p. 205). In Gawthrop's view, "the predominant operational characteristic of the fusion of democracy and bureaucracy—that which, in turn, defines our deeply ingrained paradigm of policy and administration in a democratic society—is hypocrisy" (p. 206).

Gawthrop presents as evidence of this hypocrisy our national embrace of "the democratic rhetoric of Jefferson while continuing to act in a pragmatic manner befitting Madison" (p. 206). We "continue to sanctify the virtue of union—unity through diversity—but, by the same token, we are loath to forego rugged individualism as the categorical imperative of freedom" (p. 206). The significance of these dichotomies for public administrators "who must operate in this convoluted system of democratic values and who must, at the same time, recognize the intrinsic values of bureaucracy and its attendant canons of management" is that "the art of pretense, the methods of acting or of playing a role—indeed, of wearing a mask—become virtual prerequisites for a successful career" (p. 206). One of the important outcomes of this hypocrisy, moreover, concerns contemporary thinking on public sector ethics, which Gawthrop argues "is virtually uniform in its support of the notion that the scrupulous avoidance of the wrong is tantamount to fulfilling the right, and that the qualitative values of democratic responsibility can be satisfied by adhering to the mechanistic minutiae of procedure" (p. 206).

Gawthrop also maintains that, given the utility of pretense in enabling a public administrator to appear to fulfill the demands of service, "many public administrators have sought to link their commitment of service to the amoral pretense of detached objectivity, neutral competence, and dispassionate rationality" (p. 208). The result, according to Gawthrop, is a neutered and dysfunctional public service. Indeed, he contends that in the past forty years, "the notion of administrative neutrality devolved into a programmed—that is, habituated—response that contaminated the democratic process by transfusing a bitter unreality into the lifeblood of the common good" (p. 209). In the end, however, Gawthrop suggests that a contrary view can be persuasive. He argues that public administrators who operate in a holistic system of democratic values, virtues, and vision, and who assume an integral role in contributing to the ultimate utility of democracy, cannot reasonably be expected "to detach themselves from this teleological vision" (p. 209). "In this context, objective neutrality and subjective detachment become dysfunctional attributes of administrative behavior" (p. 209).

Again, the bureaucracy–democracy dilemma, as presented in the literature, consists of two sets of contending values. Whether it concerns pluralism versus efficiency, bureaucracy as indispensable but a threat to democracy, or the challenges of control, including principal–agent relations, the bureaucracy–democracy dilemma, like the bureaucratic ethos–democratic ethos, is generally described as a clash of irreconcilable perspectives, admitting of no resolution. While Yates, Lindblom, Long, and Gawthrop allude to the possibility of common ground between the values of bureaucracy and democracy, and Wood and Waterman as well as Gruber identify several interests shared by bureaucrats and elected officials, this line of reasoning has remained relatively underdeveloped. What has also been missing is the delineation of any explicit moral basis for a reconciliation of these allegedly conflicting values. In the next section, we aim to show how our integrated ethical perspective provides such a basis through its adumbration of moral agency in public administration.

Moral Agency in Public Administration

Imagine a play about the bureaucracy–democracy dilemma. Bureaucracy is a distant and forbidding character, behind a curtain like the Wizard of Oz, while democracy is Everyman or woman, like Dorothy, the Cowardly Lion, the Scarecrow, and the Tin Man, essentially good, questing for purpose, trying to understand, often confused, coping with life's challenges, for whom everything turns out reasonably well in the end. As an individual, the bureaucrat fills the role of the redeemable villain and the citizen or elected official is the flawed hero. Taken together, these *dramatis personae* embody the central irony of American governance: Although suspicious—even evil—characters, bureaucracy and bureaucrats are vital to democracy. They help to keep politicians honest and the political process fair, while serving as targets of oversight and occasional opprobrium from those same politicians and citizens. Irony, conflict, and contradiction characterize the bureaucracy–democracy dilemma, as reflected in the literature reviewed here. For example, Yates and Gawthrop envision government as potentially both democratic and efficient but see conflict arising from our limited understanding of the balance of power between bureaucrats and experts, on the one hand, and citizens and politicians, on the other; the grafting of management canons onto democratic values; and the general fusion of bureaucratic and democratic principles, perspectives, and processes. Similarly, Etzioni-Halevy captures this irony in her description of bureaucracy as a threat to but indispensable for democracy. At the same time, however, her depiction of bureaucracy as the nonpartisan allocator of resources appears limited, if not naive, if it is meant to convey the idea that need or entitlement as a criterion for allocation is not politically determined. In any event, bureaucracy as a necessary evil is central to our current conceptualization of governance.

A corollary to this theme, however, is the notion that democracy and bureaucracy are reconcilable, at least in principle, given proper perspectives and processes. Yates believes that government should be both democratic and efficient; Lindblom proposes bargaining and mutual adjustment as a means for reconciliation; Long claims that both democratic and administrative values can be served; and Gawthrop writes of administrators who operate in a holistic system of democratic values, virtues, and visions and assume an integral role in the democratic process. Thus, although the conflict between bureaucracy and democracy has been central to the theory and practice of American governance, there has been some recognition of the potential for resolution and reconciliation. More specifically, Wood and Waterman, as well as Gruber, outline promising approaches to the dilemma in their respective models of agency theory and control-as-exchange. Both recognize in principal–agent relations the possibility, indeed the probability in some cases, of shirking, uncertainty, information asymmetry, and self-interest, and both propose specific steps to address these realities. We, too, believe that recognition of common concerns about relationships, reputation, resources, and responsibility by both principals and agents is vital to the reconciliation of the bureaucracy–democracy dilemma, and we also believe that such recognition is critical for the formulation of practical moral agency in public administration.

We have argued that our integrated objective ethics constitutes an underlying moral unity in human nature, which, if allowed to rise to consciousness, can provide both a moral foundation and moral legitimacy for the public service. It also can provide the basis for reconciliation of the dichotomous thought that has characterized public administration, in particular, and bureaucracy and democracy, in general. Such reconciliation, in our view, is crucial to the moral maturation, political efficacy, and administrative effectiveness of citizens, elected officials, and bureaucrats. By harmonizing these dichotomies, we can introduce into our governance system a new level of integrity and understanding, which in turn will be reflected in more authentic, autonomous, and accountable dialogue, decisions, and actions. The corrosive hypocrisy, pretense, and cynicism Gawthrop describes gradually will be replaced by moral coherence, confidence, and conviction. On the other hand, if our integrated objective ethics seems vaguely appealing, but abstract, remote, and improbable, especially to seasoned and scarred practitioners, we invite you to consider your own assumptions about human nature, the purpose of government, and your place in the system. If you believe that the "real world" is a totally desirable place, that it is immutable, and that you want to continue to live there, then you may see the prospect of moral agency in public administration as just another academic fantasy. If, however, you have some notion that, perhaps, no one's interest is ultimately served by artifice, deception, and ethics-as-legalism, then you may find some merit in the concept of practical moral agency, particularly as it may apply to you and your organization.

We believe that the creation of practical moral agency requires a reconceptualization of principal–agent relations. Attenuated or truncated though our democratic process may be, the moral agent acknowledges that, in the larger society, it still trumps administration in terms of perceived political legitimacy. This, however, does not necessarily translate into greater moral legitimacy. Under present circumstances, therefore, comprehensive and consistent concern with constitutional and moral values, ironically, may need to be articulated chiefly by the bureaucracy—one of the paradoxes in American governance. At the same time, moreover, the moral agent, in accordance with Wood and Waterman's recommendation, seeks to alter principal–agent relations in several ways, including extending oversight to the principal, meaning elected officials and, perhaps, even citizens, if oversight encompasses general responsibility. Although undoubtedly difficult, this effort conforms to Wamsley's notion of the public administrator as a guardian of constitutional values and the public interest. The difference here, of course, is that it is the moral agent steeped in the integrated objective ethics who is playing the guardian role, as opposed to a public administrator claiming a special place in governance based on expertise or position. With the integrated objective ethics underpinning the moral agent's thought and action, she can undertake this effort with a measure of courage and conviction; and whatever the outcome, it seems preferable, in Gawthrop's words, to wearing a mask.

The groundwork for reconciling bureaucracy and democracy and for reconceptualizing principal–agent relations has been laid by Gary Wamsley and his colleagues in Blacksburg, Virginia. For example, their 1992 essay, "A Legitimate Role for Bureaucracy in Democratic Governance," summarizes their position. After reviewing the pluralist democracy and administrative efficiency models presented by Yates, Wamsley *et al.* (1992) point out that despite the "devastating critiques" leveled against them, these models remain "battered-but-intact embodiments of conventional wisdom" (p. 63). They note that a single intellectual blow is unlikely to shatter ideologies or models, and they describe their essay "as a part of an incremental chipping and reshaping of the way we think about these issues" (p. 63). They also acknowledge the scholarly work that falls between the two models, namely, the bureaucratic politics school in political science and the work on complex organizations in sociology, but they argue that this work has not taken us far enough to alter ideologies and conventional wisdom. They maintain that more is required "if a legitimate role is to be found for the public administration in governing modern America" (p. 64). They also suggest that "[c]onsidering the development of a legitimate role for bureaucracy in democratic governance requires us to confront several things," including "[o]ur resistance to the idea of governance," as opposed to the notion of an automatic society; "[o]ur discomfort in admitting a legitimate role in governance for administration"; the limitations of pluralist democracy and administrative efficiency in regard to "how to govern a bureaucratic republic with a reasonable degree of democracy and efficiency"; and our knowledge that the work in bureaucratic politics and organizational analysis "remains largely inert for lack of normative content" (p. 65).

Among the key points made by Wamsley *et al.* are that three different value premises need to be adopted in the development of a normative framework for a bureaucratic role in governance: (1) Public administration is a social asset, not a social liability or a threat; (2) public administration is distinct from private management, the difference residing in their respective norms; and (3) there are positive aspects to the agency perspective. Agencies are repositories of specialized knowledge and historical experience, and they represent some degree of consensus as to the public interest relevant to particular societal functions. Wamsley and his colleagues also note that, among public administrators, the means of governance have taken precedence over transcendent purposes and the moral commitment to community building or the enhancement of freedom and dignity. Whereas the means are essential to claims of expertise and concerns about professional status, the trustee role for public administrators has been eroded as a result. Finally, Wamsley and his co-authors explore the constitutional role of public administrators, arguing that the Federalist interpretation of the Constitution encouraged and anticipated public administration and its role in governance. Although scholars and practitioners have emphasized nonpartisan instrumentalism, "it is neither well-grounded in the Constitution nor adequate to the demands for governance in the late twentieth century" (p. 75). On the contrary, public administration must perceive itself and be perceived by others as part of a covenant, a solemn agreement "to serve the public with competence directed toward the public interest and the maintenance of a democratic process of governance" (p. 76). Public administrators are trustees of the constitutional order that the framers intended as an expression of the will of the people.

We believe that the work of Wamsley and his co-authors represents a significant advance toward a reconciliation of the bureaucracy–democracy dilemma and a reconceptualization of principal–agent relations. We share their concern about redefining the role of public administration in our constitutional system, and like them, we believe that essential to this redefinition is broad acceptance of public administration as a social asset, rather than a social liability or threat to democracy. We maintain, however, that their work lacks a critical element, namely, an explicit moral foundation. Therefore, our aim is to augment the Blacksburg Manifesto with our integrated objective ethics, which can provide the moral basis for the development of a normative public administration framework. Moral agency in public administration and the Blacksburg Manifesto, together, are the vital ingredients for this framework. They direct our attention to the attainment of moral and political legitimacy in the governance of a bureaucratic–democratic unity grounded in constitutional values. Without first establishing moral legitimacy, however, administrative legitimacy in governance seems unlikely. Citizens, elected officials, and judges must see public administrators as their moral equals and as moral partners if the trustee role for public administrators is to be enacted.

Animated by the integrated objective ethics and committed to a new normative identity for public administration, the moral agent approaches management and policy issues with coherence, clarity, and conviction, as opposed to the fragmented, short-sighted, and self-interested thinking that is often characterized as realism. The moral agent makes a conscious and consistent effort to consider the moral dimensions, implications, and foreseeable consequences of all the decisions and actions in which she is involved. As a moral agent, she directs her energy to the creation of common ground and collaboration with her principals, both citizens and elected officials, to whom moral agency would apply as well, as Wood and Waterman recommend. Finally, perhaps we can say of moral agency what John Rohr (1990) said of self-interest planting the seed of high-minded public service: Publius would approve.

Epilogue

Ethics in the Public Service is about connections, the natural sinews and circuits between thought and action. It presupposes an innate dialectic between our capacity and need to make moral judgments and our impulse toward moral action. One catalyzes and conditions the other in an endless interactive process. Just as deontology, teleology, and virtue are inherently united, the moral mind and the moral act are organically joined in dynamic human nature. One without the other is inconceivable. Therefore, the central aim and, we hope, achievement of Ethics in the Public Service is to raise to consciousness a fundamental structural unity embedded in the human psyche and spirit, a unity which, when acknowledged, confounds the tendency toward superficial dichotomy and division.

The tortuous path between administrative thought and action is paralleled by our own collaboration on Ethics in the Public Service. The challenge of blending disciplinary perspectives is well known in the academic world, which is itself divided and which tends to resist inter-disciplinary cooperation. Even under the most collegial of circumstances, holistic or interdisciplinary approaches can be discouraged by the magnitude and complexity of scholarly subject matter. Yet, in good faith and with enduring commitment to our project, we managed to steer through our own confusion and uncertainty, as well as that of others, to discern heretofore hidden theoretical and disciplinary links, and to arrive at the unified construct called the moral mind. Our course in writing this book, therefore, was similar to the course of the practitioner struggling to weave seemingly disparate theoretical and empirical strands together into something that resembles a coherent, realistic, and responsible action plan. While our respective products may be different, the process was very much the same.

Like the practitioner, we are interested in outcomes, the results that might be achieved by activating and applying *Ethics in the Public Service.* One might say that this is the *telos* of our project. We believe that one of the outcomes might be an enlivened and enriched ethics education regimen that transcends parochial legalism and seriously delves into the principles, purposes, and personality of the public service. It would be an ethics education predicated on the underlying moral unity elaborated in this book, rather than the moral minimalism that is often packaged and purchased as substantive ethics training. Ideally, it would be an ethics education program involving citizens and elected officials as well as administrators—indeed, anyone interested in the quality and character of governance.

Ethics in the Public Service presumes and promotes integrity in the face of complexity. It embraces the power and promise of moral agency grounded in the objective, flexible, and usable ethics propounded in this book, and it offers a firm foundation on which to build a morally clear, coherent, and consistent public service. Yet, while some scholars may agree with Plato that moral knowledge necessarily entails moral character and behavior, we are mindful that knowledge alone may lack such power. We believe that those who seriously contemplate moral issues will naturally develop an appreciation for the moral good; however, it is quite possible that an agent may know the moral course of action and choose an immoral alternative. Complete moral development entails not only knowing what one should do but also having the motivation and strength to do what is right.

Finally, both subjectivists and objectivists should welcome our position because it avoids the most severe difficulties that each finds in the other. The objectivist is troubled by a moral emptiness in a subjectivism that leaves moral decisions to arbitrary, ill-defined, and unsupported feelings and opinions. The subjectivist is troubled by an apparent rigidity in an objectivism that removes individual judgment and discretion. Our position avoids both problems. We provide a structure that guides the moral reasoning process and avoids the arbitrary. Yet, while the structure guides moral agents, it does not specify how each case should be decided. We leave to the individual moral agent the means of determining how the integrated moral perspective might apply in particular instances. Thus, we reject obedience to formulaic rules, promote individual judgment, and acknowledge reasonable disagreement among those who interpret specific cases differently. We provide a means of deciding upon and justifying moral judgments without dictating them—and at least the moral question will be asked.

REFERENCES

Alway, J. 1995. *Critical Theory and Political Possibilites: Conceptions of Emancipatory Politics in the Works of Horkheimer, Adorno, Marcuse, and Habermas.* Westport, CT: Greenwood Press.

Arendt, H. 1982. *Lectures on Kant's Political Philosophy,* ed. R. Beiner. Chicago: University of Chicago Press.

Aristotle. 1956. *Metaphysics,* ed. and trans. J. Warrington. London: J. M. Dent.

———. 1980. *The Nichomachean Ethics.* D. Ross, trans. Oxford: Oxford University Press.

Auxter, T. 1982. *Kant's Moral Teleology.* Macon, GA: Mercer University Press.

Bailey, S. K. 1964. Ethics and the Public Service. *Public Administration Review.* 24:234–243.

Baron, M. W. 1995. *Kantian Ethics Almost Without Apology.* Ithaca, NY: Cornell University Press.

Bentham, J. 1970. *An Introduction to the Principles of Morals and Legislation,* ed. J. H. Burns and H. L. A. Hart. London: Athlone.

Blackburn, S. 1996. *The Oxford Dictionary of Philosophy.* New York: Oxford University Press.

Blackham, H. J. 1961. *Six Existentialist Thinkers.* London: Routledge & Kegan Paul.

Bloom, A. 1987. *The Closing of the American Mind.* New York: Simon and Schuster.

Box, R. C. 1995. Critical Theory and the Paradox of Discourse. *American Review of Public Administration.* 25:1–19.

Brandt, R. 1983. The Real and Alleged Problems of Utilitarianism. *Hastings Center Report.* 13:37–43.

Brentano, F. 1971. *The True and the Evident.* R. Chisholm, trans. London: Routledge & Kegan Paul.

Buber, M. 1956. *Writings.* J. Herberg, trans. New York: Meridian Books.

Burke, J. P. 1989. Reconciling Public Administration and Democracy: The Role of the Responsible Administrator. *Public Administration Review.* 49:180–185.

Camus, A. 1957 *L'etranger.* Paris: Gallimard.

Chandler, R. C. 1994. Deontological Dimensions of Administrative Ethics. In *Handbook of Administrative Ethics*, ed. T. L. Cooper, 147–156. New York: Marcel Dekker, Inc.

Cleary, R. E. 1989. Response to John Burke. *Public Administration Review.* 49:186.

Cooper, T. L. 1987. Hierarchy, Virtue, and the Practice of Public Administration: A Perspective for Normative Ethics. *Public Administration Review.* 47:320–328.

———. 1990. *The Responsible Administrator,* 3rd ed. San Francisco: Jossey-Bass Publishers.

———. 1991. *An Ethic of Citizenship for Public Administration.* Englewood Cliffs, NJ: Prentice Hall.

Cooper, T. L. and N. D. Wright, eds. 1992. *Exemplary Public Administrators.* San Francisco: Jossey-Bass Publishers.

Delfgaauw, B. 1969. *Twentieth Century Philosophy.* N. D. Smith, trans. Albany, NY: Magi Books.

Denhardt, K. G. 1988. *The Ethics of Public Service.* New York: Greenwood Press.

———. 1989. The Management of Ideals: A Political Perspective on Ethics. *Public Administration Review.* 49:187–193.

———. 1991. Unearthing the Moral Foundations of Public Administration: Honor, Benevolence, and Justice. In *Ethical Frontiers in Public Management,* ed. J. S. Bowman, 91–113. San Francisco: Jossey-Bass Publishers.

———. 1994. Character Ethics and the Transformation of Governance. *International Journal of Public Administration.* 17:2165–2193.

Denhardt, R. B. 1981a. *In the Shadow of Organization.* Lawrence, KS: University Press of Kansas.

———. 1981b. Toward a Critical Theory of Public Organization. *Public Administration Review.* 41:628–635.

———. 1984 *Theories of Public Organization.* Monterey, CA: Brooks/Cole Publishing Company.

———. 1990. Public Administration Theory: The State of the Discipline. In *Public Administration: The State of the Discipline,* eds. N. B. Lynn and A. Wildavsky, 43–72. Chatham, NJ: Chatham House Publishers, Inc.

Denhardt, R. B. and K. G. Denhardt. 1979. Public Administration and the Critique of Domination. *Administration & Society.* 11:107–120.

Dobel, J. P. 1990. Integrity in the Public Service. *Public Administration Review.* 50:354–366.

———. 1998. Political Prudence and the Ethics of Leadership. *Public Administration Review.* 58:74–81.

Dunn, W. N., and B. Fozouni. 1976. *Toward a Critical Administrative Theory.* Beverly Hills, CA: Sage Publications.

Edie, J. 1987. *Husserl's Phenomenology: A Critical Commentary.* Bloomington, IN: Indiana University Press.

Etzioni-Halevy, E. 1983. *Bureaucracy and Democracy: A Political Dilemma.* London: Routledge & Kegan Paul.

Fishkin, J. S. 1984. *Beyond Subjective Morality: Ethical Reasoning and Political Philosophy.* New Haven: Yale University Press.

Foot, P. 1959. Moral Beliefs. *Proceedings of the Aristotelian Society, 1958–59.* 59:83–104.

Forester, J. 1983. Critical Theory and Organizational Analysis. In *Beyond Method: Strategies for Social Research,* ed. G. Morgan, 234–246. Beverly Hills, CA: Sage Publications.

Fox, C. J. 1989. Free to Choose, Free to Win, Free to Lose: The Phenomenology of Ethical Space. *International Journal of Public Administration.* 6:913–930.

———. 1994. The Use of Philosophy in Administrative Ethics. In *Handbook of Administrative Ethics,* ed. T. L. Cooper, 83–105. New York: Marcel Dekker, Inc.

Fox, C. J. and H. T. Miller. 1995. *Postmodern Public Administration: Toward Discourse.* Thousand Oaks, CA: Sage Publications.

Frankena, W. K. 1963. *Ethics.* Englewood Cliffs, NJ: Prentice Hall.

Frederickson, H. G. 1972. Toward a New Public Administration. In *Toward a New Public Administration,* ed. F. Marini, 309–331. Scranton: Chandler Publications.

———. 1997. *The Spirit of Public Administration.* San Francisco: Jossey-Bass Publishers.

Gawthrop, L. C. 1997. Democracy, Bureaucracy, and Hypocrisy Redux: A Search for Sympathy and Compassion. *Public Administration Review.* 57:205–210.

Gruber, J. E. 1987. *Controlling Bureaucracies: Dilemmas in Democratic Governance.* Berkeley: University of California Press.

Guy, M. E. 1991. Using High Reliability Management to Promote Ethical Decision Making. In *Ethical Frontiers in Public Management,* ed. J. S. Bowman, 185–204. San Francisco: Jossey-Bass Publishers.

Habermas, J. 1995. *Moral Consciousness and Communicative Action.* C. Lenhardt and W. Nicholsen, trans. Cambridge, MA: MIT Press.

Hare, R. M. 1952. *The Language of Morals.* Oxford: Clarendon Press.

———. 1976. Ethical Theory and Utilitarianism. In *Contemporary Ethics,* ed. J. P. Sterba, 190–201. Englewood Cliffs, NJ: Prentice Hall.

Harmon, M. M. 1972. Normative Theory and Public Administration: Some Suggestions for a Redefinition of Public Responsibility. In *Toward a New Public Administration,* ed. F. Marini, 172–185. Scranton: Chandler Publications.

———. 1995. *Responsibility as Paradox.* Thousand Oaks, CA: Sage Publications.

Harmon, M. M. and R. T. Mayer. 1986. *Organization Theory for Public Administration.* Boston: Little, Brown and Company.

Hart, D. K. 1984. The Virtuous Citizen, the Honorable Bureaucrat, and "Public Administration." *Public Administration Review.* 44:111–120.

———. 1994. Administration and the Ethics of Virtue: In All Things, Choose First for Good Character and Then for Technical Expertise. In *Handbook of Administrative Ethics*, ed. T. L. Cooper, 107–123. New York: Marcel Dekker, Inc.

Heidegger, M. 1977. *Basic Writings from Being and Time to the Task of Thinking*. New York: Harper and Row.

Hill, J. 1976. *The Ethics of G. E. Moore: A New Interpretation*. Amsterdam: Van Gorcum.

Hume, D. 1951. *A Treatise on Human Nature*, ed. L. A. Selby. London: Oxford University Press.

Hummel, R. P. 1990. Uncovering Validity Criteria for Stories Managers Hear and Tell. *American Review of Public Administration*. 20:303–314.

———. 1991. Stories Managers Tell: Why They Are as Valid as Science. *Public Administration Review*. 51:31–41.

Husserl, E. 1964. *The Idea of Phenomenology*. W. P. Alston and G. Nakhnikian, trans. The Hague: Nijhoff.

Jos, P. H. 1988. Moral Autonomy and the Modern Organization. *Polity*. 21:321–343.

———. 1990. Administrative Responsibility Revisited: Moral Consensus and Moral Autonomy. *Administration & Society*. 22:228–248.

Kant, I. 1949. *Critique of Practical Reason*, ed. and trans., L. W. Beck. Chicago: University of Chicago Press.

———. 1965. *Critique of Pure Reason*. N. K. Smith, trans. New York: St. Martin's Press.

———. 1970. The Metaphysics of Morals. In *Kant's Political Writings*. H. B. Nisbett, trans. Cambridge, UK: Cambridge University Press.

———. 1970. Perpetual Peace. In *Kant's Political Writings*. H. B. Nisbett, trans. Cambridge, UK: Cambridge University Press.

———. 1989. *Fundamental Principles of the Metaphysics of Morals*. T. K. Abbott, trans. New York: Macmillan.

———. 1991. *Metaphysics of Morals*. M. McGregor, trans. Cambridge, UK: Cambridge University Press.

Kass, H. D. 1989. Exploring Agency as a Basis for Ethical Theory in Public Administration. *International Journal of Public Administration*. 12:949–969.

———. 1990. Stewardship as a Fundamental Element in Images of Public Administration. In *Images and Identities in Public Administration*, eds. H. D. Kass and B. L. Catron, 113–131. Newbury Park, CA: Sage Publicaitons.

———. 1994. Trust, Agency, and Institution Building in Contemporary American Democracy. *Administrative Theory and Praxis*. 16:15–30.

Kierkegaard, S. 1946. *A Kierkegaard Anthology*, ed. R. Bretall. Princeton: Princeton University Press.

———. 1958. *The Journals of Kierkegaard*. A. Dru, trans. London: Collins.

Kirkhart, L. 1972. Toward a New Theory of Public Administration. In *Toward a New Public Administration*, ed. F. Marini, 127–164. Scranton: Chandler Publications.

Kolenda, K. 1990. *Rorty's Humanistic Pragmatism.* Tampa: University of South Florida Press.

Kronenberg, P. 1972. The Scientific and Moral Authority of Empirical Theory of Public Administration. In *Toward a New Public Administration,* ed. F. Marini, 190–225. Scranton: Chandler Publications.

Lewis, C. W. 1991. *The Ethics Challenge in Public Service.* San Francisco: Jossey-Bass Publishers.

MacIntyre, A. 1981. *After Virtue.* Notre Dame, IN: Notre Dame University Press.

Marcel, G. 1969. *The Philosophy of Existence.* M. Harari, trans. Freeport, NY: Books for Libraries Press.

Marini, F. 1994. Echoes from No-person's Land: Reflections on the Political Theory of Some Recent Dialogue. *Administrative Theory and Praxis.* 16:1–15.

McCarthy, T. 1979. *The Critical Theory of Jurgen Habermas.* Cambridge, MA: MIT Press.

Meier, K. J. 1997. Bureaucracy and Democracy: The Case for More Bureaucracy and Less Democracy. *Public Administration Review.* 57:193–199.

Merleau-Ponty, M. 1973. *Adventures of the Dialectic.* J. Bein, trans. Evanston, IL: Northwestern University Press.

Mill, J. S. 1979. *Utilitarianism,* ed. G. Sher. Indianapolis: Hackett Publishing.

Moore, G. E. 1966. The Subject Matter of Ethics. In *Twentieth Century Philosophy: The Analytic Tradition,* ed. M. Weitz. Toronto: Collier McMillan.

———. 1951. *Principia Ethica.* Cambridge, UK: Cambridge University Press.

Nietzsche, F. 1968. *Basic Writings of Nietzsche,* ed. and trans. W. Kaufmass. New York: Modern Library.

Paynter, J. 1972. Comment: On a Redefinition of Administrative Responsibility. In *Toward a New Public Administration,* ed. F. Marini, 185–189. Scranton: Chandler Publications.

Place, U. T. 1966. Consciousness is Just Brain Process. In *Body, Mind, and Death,* ed. A. Flew. New York: Macmillan.

Plato. 1910. *Platonis Euthyphro,* ed. J. Adam. Cambridge, UK: Cambridge University Press.

———. 1991. *The Republic of Plato,* ed. and trans., A. Bloom. New York: HarperCollins.

Pops, G. M. 1994. A Teleological Approach to Administrative Ethics. In *Handbook of Administrative Ethics,* ed. T. L. Cooper, 157–166. New York: Marcel Dekker, Inc.

Pugh, D. L. 1991. The Origins of Ethical Frameworks in Public Administration. In *Ethical Frontiers in Public Management,* ed. J. S. Bowman, 9–33. San Francisco: Jossey-Bass Publishers.

Rawls, J. 1955. Two Concepts of Rules. *Philosophical Review.* 64:3–32.

———. 1971. *A Theory of Justice.* Cambridge, MA: Harvard University Press.

Reiss, H. 1970. Introduction. In *Kant's Political Writings*. H. B. Nisbett, trans. Cambridge, UK: Cambridge University Press.

Riley, P. 1983. *Kant's Political Philosophy*. Totowa, NJ: Rowman and Littlefield.

Rohr, J. A. 1989. *Ethics for Bureaucrats: An Essay on Law and Values*, 2nd ed. New York: Marcel Decker, Inc.

———. 1990. The Constitutional Case for Public Administration. In *Refounding Public Administration*, eds. G. L. Wamsley, *et. al.*, 52–95. Newbury Park, CA: Sage Publications.

Rorty, R. 1989. *Contingency, Irony, and Solidarity*. New York: Cambridge University Press.

———. 1991. *Objectivity, Relativism, and Truth*. Cambridge, UK: Cambridge University Press.

Rosen, A. D. 1993. *Kant's Theory of Justice*. Ithaca, NY: Cornell University Press.

Sartre, J-P. 1947. *Existentialism*. B. Frechtman, trans. New York: Philosophical Library.

———. 1974. *Being and Nothingness*. H. Barnes, trans. Secaucus, NJ: Citadel Press.

Schmidtz, D. 1995. *Rational Choice and Moral Agency*. Princeton: Princeton University Press.

Selznick, P. 1992. *The Moral Commonwealth*. Berkeley: University of California Press.

Singer, M. G. 1961. *Generalization in Ethics*. New York: Alfred A. Knopf.

Smart, J. J. 1971. Sensations and Brain Processes. In *Materialism and the Mind-Body Problem*, ed. D. M. Rosenthal. Englewood Cliffs, NJ: Prentice Hall.

Stewart, D. W. 1984. Managing Competing Claims: An Ethical Framework for Human Resource Decision Making. *Public Administration Review*. 44:14–23.

Sullivan, R. J. 1991. *Immanuel Kant's Moral Theory*. Cambridge, UK: Cambridge University Press.

Tillich, P. 1965. *Ultimate Concern: Tillich in Dialogue*, ed. D. M. Brown. New York: Harper and Row.

Ventriss, C. 1987. Two Critical Issues of American Public Administration. *Administration & Society*. 19:25–47.

Wamsley, G. L. 1990. The Agency Perspective: Public Administrators as Agential Leaders. In *Refounding Public Administration*, eds. G. L. Wamsley, *et al.*, 114–162. Newbury Park, CA: Sage Publications.

Wamsley, G. L., Charles T. Goodsell, John A. Rohr, Orion White, and James Wolf. 1992. A Legitimate Role for Bureaucracy in Democratic Governance. In *The State of Public Bureaucracy*, ed. L. B. Hill, 59–86. Armonk, NY: M. E. Sharpe, Inc.

Warnock, M. 1986. *Existentialism*. New York: Oxford University Press.

White, J. D. 1986. On the Growth of Knowledge in Public Administration. *Public Administration Review*. 46:15–24.

———. 1990. Images of Administrative Reason and Rationality: The Recovery of

Practical Discourse. In *Images and Identities in Public Administration*, eds. H. D. Kass and B. L. Catron, 132–150. Newbury Park, CA: Sage Publications.

———. 1992. Knowledge Development and Use in Public Administration: Views from Postpositivism, Poststructuralism, and Postmodernism. In *Public Management in an Interconnected World: Essays in the Minnowbrook Tradition*, eds. M. T. Bailey and R. T. Mayer, 159–176. New York: Greenwood Press.

White, O. F. and C. J. McSwain. 1990. The Phoenix Project: Raising a New Image of Public Administration from the Ashes of the Past. In *Images and Identities in Public Administration*, eds. H. D. Kass and B. L. Catron, 23–59. Newbury Park, CA: Sage Publications.

Woller, G. M. and K. D. Patterson. 1997. Public Administration Ethics: A Postmodern Perspective. *American Behavioral Scientist*. 41:103–118.

Wood, B. D. and R. W. Waterman. 1994. *Bureaucratic Dynamics: The Role of Bureaucracy in a Democracy*. Boulder: Westview Press.

Yates, D. 1982. *Bureaucratic Democracy: The Search for Democracy and Efficiency in American Government*. Cambridge: Harvard University Press.

INDEX